# The Ultimate Europe
# Train Travel Guide
## A *BlueMarbleXpress*
## *Explore the World Vacation Series*

by J. Doyle White

# Table of Contents

# Introduction

Traveling by train is such a wonderful experience, and in Europe it is so incredibly easy to do. You can literally see all of Europe and even travel into Asia all aboard a train. If you plan your trip just right, you can schedule the stops in locations you want to visit or plan a trip aboard a sleeper car and relax for the evening, waking up to a beautiful, new European location.

This guide includes a comprehensive list of European train stations (and there are many) listed by country in alphabetic order. This guide will help you plan your European trip accordingly with all the information you will need to find the trian stations. You will also find all the pertinent information about the correct papers and all the items necessary to travel legally and comfortably throughout Europe.

The highlight of the guide is a description of the many wonderful rail journeys you can take if you'd like a pre-planned itinerary. You will discover the manmade and natural wonders of Europe as you read through the pages of this comprehensive guide.

# A Map of Train Stations in Europe

Source[1]

---

[1] en.wikipedia.org/wiki/File:Magistrale_for_Europe.gif

# Section 1 – Traveling Through Europe by Train

Train Travel has a very strong stigma attached to it in most parts of the world, but in Europe traveling by train is an exciting mix of luxury, peace of mind, and a sense of adventure.

While you may have never traveled by train before in your own country or when visiting others, the minute you set foot in any one of the European countries bid farewell to the ever-smiling cabin attendants because you will find trains to be the perfect mode of transportation here. Why? Aside from the fact that the European train network is dense, dependable, and convenient, why would you want to miss a view of the beautiful landscapes and lush, green sceneries welcoming you to this wonderland?

Train travel is a much cheaper option for traveling to multiple European countries in one go. While there is a lot of hassle involved in getting to the airport, passing security, waiting for hours, and finally boarding an international flight, all you have to do to travel via train is arrive 30 minutes early, show your ticket, and pick a seat! Moreover, train travel is the best way to familiarize yourself with local cultures of the surrounding regions, mingle with natives, and, at the same time, forget all worries related to driving in a foreign country, following road rules, or even having your luggage rummaged through by security officials!

Because of the increasing number of passengers choosing to travel Europe by train, authorities have pushed up services by notches. Frequent stops and departures, flexible plans, long-term passes, and comfortable seating and dining are just some of the facilities you will find in state-of-the-art European trains.

# Travel Documents and Visa Requirements

Even though it seems quite easy to go from Italy to Greece via train, in reality you will be crossing an international boundary to enter another sovereign state. The European Union is one region where visa policies and frontier restrictions are quite lax, making it very easy for tourists and independent travelers to move back and forth in order to explore the wonders of Europe.

Despite this ease, a certain level of preparation has to be done before traveling internationally. How much you have to prepare depends on a number of factors: two of the most prominent ones are discussed below.

- **Purpose of Visit:** Why are you visiting Europe? Is it for leisure, work, or visiting family members, or for immigration purposes? The reason for your visit dictates how you will prepare for European travel. The documents needed, the length of time required for preparation, and the extent of caution are all determinants that will be decided upon once you state the purpose of travel

- **Duration of Visit:** How long will you be visiting for? Is the duration of your visit a few days/weeks, like a regular tourist, or will you require extensions? The visa policy of the European Union is quite unique. It has certain restrictions that limit a traveler's stay in the countries that come under its umbrella. Details regarding this will be discussed in the next few paragraphs.

Depending on these two variables, you will now plan for travel documents and visa requirements to make sure your European stay is smooth and enjoyable.

## Travel Necessities

Your nationality will largely determine the kind of travel documents you carry with you. If you are a non-EU citizen, carrying your passport is a must at all times. This passport should be valid for at least 6 months after the date of return from the EU. Therefore, before you apply for visas, make sure you have a valid passport and it has all your personal details correctly written down.

On the other hand, if you are an EU citizen, you can even travel within Europe with only an ID card on you. Because many EU countries have no solid frontiers, border control authorities do not require any more authentication from citizens of these countries. However, all these details are valid only when you travel to Europe for tourism and leisure. If your purpose is business or study, relevant documents justifying your stay will be needed.

Within the EU, a Schengen Region has been formed by 25 countries known as the Schengen Countries. These include Austria, Belgium, Czech Republic, Denmark, Estonia, Finland, France, Germany, Greece, Hungary, Iceland, Italy, Latvia, Lithuania, Luxembourg, Malta, Netherlands, Norway, Poland, Portugal, Slovakia, Slovenia, Spain, Sweden, and Switzerland.

According to the Schengen Agreement, a traveler can move between these 25 countries easily if he has a Schengen Visa. Such a visa is a pass into all EU countries, with the exception of the United Kingdom and Ireland because they are not part of the Schengen Agreement. Hence, if you want to travel across Europe freely, with minimum legal hassle, all you have to do is get a Schengen Visa on your passport. Every time you cross a border, your Non-EU passport will be checked and this visa allowance will let you into the Schengen country of your choice.

Because Europe is a popular tourism destination, acquiring a Schengen Visa from most countries is quite easy. It can take between 2 to 10 working days for the visa to be approved and a traveler can stay for up to 90 days at a stretch in Europe with this visa, within a period of 180 days.

Apart from EU citizenship, many other nationalities are allowed in Europe without any visa. These include North American, Australian, Croatian, Japanese, and New Zealander. If you have one of these nationalities, all you have to carry with you for your European escapade is a valid passport.

While traveling within Europe is quite simple, make sure you acquire all details about entering and exiting it as a member of your home country, to avoid inconveniences and disappointments after you have already planned your trip.

## Timetables and Travel Planners

Once you have made up your mind to explore Europe by train, preparing for the trip has to be done in advance. One main advantage of choosing this mode of transport is that it allows travelers to plan trips from one country to the other very flexibly. The train network, as mentioned previously, is quite extensive throughout Europe. Not only do trains make frequent stops, they leave major capital stations every few minutes, making it very easy for tourists to reach their chosen destinations.

However, to do so, one has to be aware of a number of aspects of traveling in trains. First, there are Timetables at which trains arrive and depart and second, there are Route Planners that sketch out a complete path for your trip. Many independent travelers often feel they do not need any kind of planning when heading out to various European destinations. After all, where's the adventure if you know exactly what happens when?

While this approach may work for some, it is necessary to realize that when you are in an alien country with no knowledge of rules and regulations, Route Planners and Timetables are a cushion that ensures a comfortable time. Moreover, they also help you stay on track with the plans you have laid out for the trip. For instance, if you want to visit three countries in ten days, missing a train that only leaves once a day can be a big dent in your plans. Therefore, once you know which train to wait for and when, by all means, have as much adventure as you want!

Many websites and online forums are linked to railway network databases all across Europe. The main aim of these websites is to make travel easy for an average tourist and to help him plan the best and most fulfilling vacations, all from the comfort of his hotel room. One such website is called www.raileurope-world.com. Rail Europe World is a complete and comprehensive guide to traveling across European destinations by acquiring relevant information about train timetables and route planning.

One visit and you will see how this website lists all possible trains leaving for Paris from London on a particular date. Together with arrival and departure times, this schedule also gives daily confirmations for the same. Moreover, when you click on a given schedule, details like the services available on-board are also explained, together with the option to book or un-book your seat for this train ride.

Other online applications/websites that can come in handy are similar to the German Route Planner. These websites provide extensive guides on how to choose the best route within a county/city and between cities and countries, to enhance the traveling experience and expose a tourist to most of the European beauty and nightlife. These routes give detailed instructions on which highway to take, where to turn on an intersection, and which exit to take, so navigating across Europe becomes a piece of cake. Some other features on these websites are city guides, tourist attractions, operating train stations, and stopover points.

## Tickets

Tickets are a necessity when you decide to travel via train across Europe. Because of the popularity of this mode of transport, hundreds of different types of train tickets can be purchased and booked in advance. You will find many options in this category that a traveler should be aware of if he wants to ensure a comfortable journey.

The following topics give ample details regarding the ticketing system in Europe.

### Ticket Fare

One of the biggest factors affecting ticket fares is the type of train you choose to travel in. Several types of trains commute between different European destinations. While each is as good as the other, your choice will depend on your preferences and the amount of money you are ready to pay for the services.

For instance, if you choose Europe as *the* destination for your vacation because of the breathtaking scenery and panoramic views, hop on-board the Glacier Express that costs about 137 Euros for a ride across three to four different cities. On the other hand, if you want to go from London to Paris in a mere 2 hours, the Eurostar is your best option, with a 49 Euro ticket.

The same goes for domestic travel within Europe as well. Depending on the type of train you choose and the time of the day you want to travel at (some times are peak hours in terms of business and so-cial movements), you can find a number of options with competitive fares from local train travel as well. For instance, trains leave London for Manchester every 10 to 15 minutes daily. Ranging between 30 Euros to 170 Euros, you can schedule a trip to Manchester lasting 2 hours 10 minutes with just a few clicks.

Moreover, keep in mind that just likes plane tickets, train tickets can be bought well in advance to avail cheaper rates and discounts. Last minute booking usually costs more because the option to choose between different carriers and various times is not available. Always make sure that you plan ahead of time to get the best possible ticket fares.

## Online Booking

Gone are the days when you had to personally buy a ticket at a train station or wait for it to arrive in the mail. Today, companies that run domestic and international trains between European destinations provide an option for online booking and reservation of tickets on their websites. These and other websites like www.eurail.com and www.raileurope-world.com have separate booking and reservations sections where travelers can plug-in the dates they want to travel and receive a detailed schedule in a matter of minutes.

This schedule will display a number of options for travel time, destination, and stopovers, and—of course—ticket fare. Once you have chosen the best one, you will be asked to add this to your Shopping Cart and make an online payment. Once done, you will receive a confirmation code in your inbox, called the PNR code. With this code, you can either travel 'ticketless' or print the emailed ticket before departure!

## Rail Passes

If you plan to visit multiple destinations, Rail Passes are perhaps the most convenient way to travel across Europe. Nonetheless, the efficacy of these passes is questioned again and again by an average traveler who compares them to city-to-city tickets. So, why buy passes?

### Rail Passes vs. City–to–City Tickets

While tourists in Europe use both Rail Passes and city-to-city tickets equally, many instances justify the use of one over the other.

Rail Passes are an ideal option if you want to travel extensively, have flexible travel dates, and visit multiple destinations. Because you already have a pass, when you arrive at a train station that accepts this particular pass, you will be allowed to board without waiting in lines and going through hectic ticket purchasing procedures.

City-to-city tickets, on the other hand, are feasible when you want to travel to one or two destinations only, for a short period, and you have fixed dates of travel. If everything about your European vacation is planned and decided ahead of time, you can easily travel on city-to-city tickets.

### What Type of Rail Pass Should You Buy?

Because of the flexibility and ease they offer, Rail Passes have become quite popular among travelers who do not mind spending some extra money to have easy access to several European destinations. Before you hurry into deciding which one to purchase, ask yourself the following questions:

- How many countries do you want to visit? Many Rail Passes are country-specific (i.e., they will take you to 4 or 5 countries over a certain period of time).
- How many days do you need the pass for? All passes are valid for varying lengths of time.

- How many people are traveling? Does everyone have a pass? Different passes are valid for various age groups and train classes.

Based on this criteria, you can buy one of the following Rail Passes for your trip:

- Eurail Global Pass: Allows consecutive-day first class travel to Austria, Belgium, Croatia, Czech Republic, Denmark, Finland, France, Germany, Greece, Holland, Hungary, Italy, Luxembourg, Norway, Portugal, Republic of Ireland, Romania, Slovenia, Spain, Sweden, and Switzerland. It comes with 15 days, 21 days, 1 month, 2 month, and 3 month validity, all of which can be purchased at different prices.
- Eurail Select Pass: Allows consecutive (or non-consecutive) travel to 3,

4, or 5 selected countries over a period of 5, 6, 8, 10, or 15 days within a 2-month period.

- Multiple Country Pass: Allows travel to 2, 3, or 4 countries of your choice.
- Single Country Pass: If you want to explore only one country, opt for a single country pass to save money.
- Youth Passes: Youth passes are available for travelers between the ages of 16 and 25.

Whichever pass you choose to purchase, make sure you arrive early at the train station on the date of your first departure to validate the pass before the journey begins. Remember, validation cannot be done once you board a train, in which case your pass may be confiscated.

## Train Types and Reservations

Another important consideration to keep in mind regarding train travel across Europe is the type of train you choose. Many tourists are taken by surprise at this selection because they may have never been on board trains other than the regular domestic ones. In Europe, however, a traveler gets to choose from various types of trains, depending on his preference for time, luxury, and comfort.

The most prominent ones that will take you from country to country are:

- High Speed Trains

High Speed Trains are modern and efficient. They offer convenience and timely travel in state-of-the-art buggies that run on tracks specifically made to keep the track sounds at an absolute minimum. Hence, travelers can expect to arrive at their destinations quickly with no stopovers. Most Rail Passes like the Eurail can be used for high-speed trains. Because these trains commute between major European cities, seat reservations are mandatory.

- Night Trains

Overnight Trains are the best mode of transportation if you are traveling after sunset. Because a traveler usually spends a large part of the night in the train, these trains are also called Hotel Trains. Owing to their popularity, night trains have expanded the kind of seating/sleeping comfort they offer. Depending on your budget, you can choose to book a reclining seat, a Sleeping Cabin, Couchettes, or Sleeperettes to ensure your journey is comfortable and hassle-free. Families visiting Europe for a vacation often prefer Night Trains because long distances can be covered during the night while children are sound asleep.

- Regional Trains

Regional Trains are the most common type of transport in Europe. These trains connect large, economic hubs to small towns and villages situated between major cities. If you want to get to know a country's culture, hop on board a Regional Train and take a tour of its quiet suburbs.

- Scenic Trains

Scenic Trains are a popular choice among tourists who are in no hurry for their European vacation to end! These trains follow routes that pass some of the most beautiful meadows, countryside attractions, bridges, tunnels, and vegetation fields of European cities. A ride past breathtaking mountain scenery, lakes, and coastlines is one of the best ways to reconnect with nature and see the true beauty of this part of the world. To add to this, Scenic Trains often make stops at local sites where foreigners can witness local arts and crafts and mingle with the natives.

## Train Reservations

Making reservations is a sensible decision if you are visiting Europe in the peak seasons. Apart from the Regional Trains, every other train journey requires passengers to make reservations in advance because holding a Rail Pass does not guarantee a seat.

Reservations can be made in one of the following ways:

- Through a railway website
- Through a sales agent
- At the train station
- By phone

## Discounts

Finding discounted packages for your annual vacation is a stroke of luck. Who doesn't like to pay less and explore more? Because Europe has become one of the number one tourist destinations across the world, travel packages often come with discounts and reduced fares to encourage travelers to spend more time there and indulge in luxuries.

Generally, advance purchase and booking guarantees discounted rates, compared to last minute buying. Apart from this, many types of discounts and deals can be found; however, these deals have to be signed up for before you start traveling. Rail Europe (www.raileurope-world.com), a popular website for online booking and information for European travel, offers the following discounts and deals:

- Youth Fare: If a traveler is under 26 years of age, Rail Europe offers discounted fares on $2^{nd}$ class rail travel. From 10% to up to 36% (depending on the destination chosen), Youth Fare offers a great opportunity for youngsters to explore Europe by train. These rates also apply to Rail Passes. For instance, if the Eurail Global Pass is made on Youth Fare, the owner will qualify for a 35% discount on full fares.
- Senior Fare: Senior Fare gives old aged people an opportunity to explore Europe for very reasonable rates. This type of offer gives discounts ranging from 13% to 25% for all those citizens who are over 60 years of age and that too for $1^{st}$ class travel!

- **Friends & Family Fare:** If you are traveling as a family or group of friends, you can take advantage of Group Discounts. Some criteria for Friends & Family Discount Fares are:
  - Every member has to book tickets at the same time.
  - Every member has to travel at the same time.
  - Discounts for Children and Adults are different, each depending on age and country to be visited.
  - Typical adult fare is reduced by 15% and child fare is reduced by 50%.

Apart from these fixed discounts, avid travelers often keep a watchful eye on seasonal deals that many rail companies put up on their websites. These include anniversary sales, end of season sales, or even birthday offers. For instance, the Eurail Global Pass Free Day Promotion gives travelers 2 days off with a 15-day continuous pass, 3 days off with a 21-day continuous pass, and 5 days off with a 1-month continuous pass.

For these deals, always keep checking the Rail Europe website or any other that you use to book train tickets, to make sure you can avail the best ones as and know when they are put up.

## Accommodation

The next consideration, after the choice of transport, is accommodation. No matter which country or city you decide to visit with a Eurail Pass or a city-to-city ticket, having adequate accommodation is a must. In this regard, Europe is a haven for every traveler. Be it luxury, 5-star ac-commodation or reasonable yet comfortable Bed & Breakfasts, just about every option is easily accessible.

As mentioned previously, the mere influx of local and foreign tourists in Europe has made the hospitality industry quite active. There are several types of accommodation to choose from and all of these can be made part of the overall travel package.

- Hotels: There is no dearth of 3-, 4-, and 5-star hotels in Europe. Be it any country, city, or even a small town, excellent hotels with fully operational spas, restaurants, and bars are now a norm. Most travelers who prefer vacationing with friends and family members choose luxury hotels as part of the overall tourist package. No doubt, after a day spent exploring Europe and traveling on regional trains, a luxurious hotel is a welcoming thought.

- Youth Hostels: Youth hostels are a very convenient option for independent travelers, students, and backpackers who prefer to spend most of their time outside the accommodation. While many would cringe at the thought of staying at one, managements at these hostels have improved facilities greatly. Not only do you have to spend less on accommodation, you also get to meet people from various cultures and ethnicities in a very informal and friendly environment. www.hostelworld.com, a leading accommodation website, is the best resource for finding hostels in Europe.

- Home Exchanges: Don't like staying in hotels? Want a homely environment? Home Exchange is the option for you. With this accommodation choice, tourists live in another person's home that has been signed up for exchange. Because this option is quite common in Europe, resources like The International Home Exchange Network (www.ihen.com) have all the details you would want to think about.

- Couchsurfing: A rather peculiar accommodation, Couchsurfing, is another option to consider. With this option, a local resident of the place you are visiting agrees to become your host for the duration of the trip! The biggest advantage of couchsurfing is zero accommodation cost. Spending time around natives and seeing tourist attractions from the eyes of a local are added benefits. www.couchsurfing.org is a website that details the necessities for this accommodation.

- Camping: If you are in love with adventure and nature, camping nights will weigh heavier for you than any amount of luxury in a 5-star hotel. Camping in the suburbs and meadows of destinations like Ireland and Spain is not only common, it is a once in a lifetime experience. Check out the best camping spots across Europe on www.campingcompass.com.
- Farm Stays: Farm Stays are an excellent way to explore European countries like Spain, United Kingdom, and Italy where natural beauty is in abundance. Not only does one

get to spend time away from the hustle bustle of the city, Farm Stays help you reconnect with nature at the same time as providing all essential facilities. www.GoNomand.com is a comprehensive collection of Farm Lodgings in Europe.

## Navigating Train Stations

Train Travel is very popular in all European countries, which is why you will find train stations and stops every few miles. Be it a bustling capital, a small, humble town, or a far-flung village, regional trains will service every stop and you can travel without any hassle.

However, the mere number of train stations and their size, especially in metropolitan cities of Europe, can be daunting. A first timer can easily get lost and lose his way at a train station because at any one time, hundreds of trains leave for various destinations and many more arrive, with throngs of passengers waiting to get off the platform.

With a train to catch for your next destination, how can you be sure you are at the correct platform, looking at the train that will depart any minute? Train Station navigation is as important as planning the perfect city tour because if you get lost in either precious time and resources may be wasted. How can you navigate a train station well?

- Station Facilities

Because European Train Stations are visited by millions of people all year round, authorities have put up signs, arrows, and detailed maps every few steps to ensure visitors are guided properly. Moreover, every prominent Railway Station will also have a tourist office, where travelers can ask for information regarding arriving and departing trains, addresses for major locations across the city, etc. Other facilities include restaurants, cafés, shopping arenas, phone booths, post offices, currency exchange counters, ATMs, and luggage counters.

- Transportation To and From

Passengers coming out of train stations need not worry about transportation facilities to get to the city. Bus stands, cycle stands, rent-a-car offices, and taxis are available right outside the station so tourists can hop on any one and start vacationing!

- Finding the Right Train

At all departure and arrival platforms, you will find automated listings of all trains that stop or pass the particular station. These large, computerized boards give minute-to-minute updates about departures so passengers can keep track of time and board the right trains.

- Going To the Right Station

Tourists often get confused about the station they should arrive at to catch a regional or high-speed train. Because there are a number of stations in most metropolitan cities, one has to check in advance to make sure they arrive at the correct station. Many times the same trains leave for the same destinations from multiple stations; therefore, always check the station's name on your pass/ticket or call the tourist office for further details.

- Station Lounges

Modern and state-of-the-art train stations are just like airports. Apart from other on-site facilities, luxurious lounges are also available for 1$^{st}$ class passengers or holders of Eurail passes. Make sure you check the privileges that come with your travel package beforehand.

## 10 Ultimate Tips for Train Travel in Europe

Train Travel is not only exciting; it is a must in Europe. According to many experts and observers of the Hospitality Industry, if tourists don't travel by train even once when they visit Europe, they haven't truly experienced life in this part of the world. Fast paced and thrilling, train rides in Europe are definitely something to remember when you come back home.

To make train trips smooth and enjoyable, a number of considerations have to be kept in mind. Some tips are given below.

1. Use the Information Desk: Planning international train journeys is not a

run-of-the-mill task for many people. Information Desks at train stations are ever ready to provide much-needed information to passengers who may be using this mode of transportation for the first time. Explain the details of your travel to the agents and let them give appropriate suggestions.

2. Buying tickets: Whenever you buy train tickets, be it at the station or from a website, make sure you have all the information you need. Do not leave room for guessing or planning later. If you buy a ticket from the ticket counter, be clear whether you want to reserve a $1^{st}$ or $2^{nd}$ class seat, an overnight or day trip, and if you will be making stops or not.

3. Make use of facilities: There are many facilities on-board European

trains. Apart from basic amenities, you will also find charging sockets, clean and hygienic restrooms, bars, and cafes. However, make sure you have checked for these facilities well in advance because many regional trains that commute short distances may not carry food or have charging sockets that are more suitable for long distance traveling.

4. Always keep safety first: Safety should always be a top priority. Make sure you arrive at the station well before departure so you can board the train without being a pack of nerves! If you panic, a number of things can go wrong. Moreover, always listen carefully to the announcements on the train and at the station. Remain seated if the conductor says so, and always keep

your pass/ticket with you until the journey is over.

5. Every train has different rules: While the general safety precautions are the same for all stations, some rules are specific to train types. For instance, regional trains take you to small towns and villages that are not very developed. Therefore, use your own logic to stay safe and follow safety rules like standing away from the tracks and keeping your luggage with you at all times. On the other hand, for high-speed trains your attention should be focused on staying put when the train starts and stops so that you do not fall.

6. Be economical: Even if you have the resources, save as much money and time as possible during traveling. Boarding overnight trains for

long distance traveling is the best way to cover distances while you sleep. Since most tourists have a limited number of days on their itineraries, this tactic works well to help them explore as much of Europe as possible!

7. Train to airport: If you are scheduled for a flight back home via air travel, why not use the train one last time? Many trains run between cities and airports several times a day. If you want to keep travel cheap, take a train to the Airport Train Station that connects directly to terminals and airport lounges.

8. Shop for passes: Before purchasing a pass, shop around for one. As mentioned previously, hundreds of different Rail Passes are valid for varying durations. Moreover, each

pass has restrictions and country specifications that need to be followed before the pass is used.

9. Keep luggage safe: Keeping your belongings safe and secure is important. Even while you are sleeping during the journey, make sure valuables like money, jewels, passports, and ID cards are kept safely in inner pockets or waist belts. If you do not have accommodation, you can rent a locker for a small fee and store valuables in it.

10. Book Sleepers and Couchettes: Sleepers and Couchettes are not a given when you buy tickets. If you are traveling on an overnight train and want to relax through the night, make sure you book these in advance because they fill up fast.

# Section 2 – Historic and Scenic Railways Journeys

## The Glacier Express

The Glacier Express is a Swiss train that travels from the mountain resorts St. Mortiz and Zermatt. Against the backdrop of snowcapped peaks, it provides a picturesque scene for travelers to enjoy. The Glacier Express is rightly named for its ingenious capacity to traverse alongside snowy Alps. Fortunately for the passengers, this train is the slowest Express train designed, to allow people to view as many beautiful places en route as possible.

Another perk is that in the long journey there is a provision for one seat per passenger, to enhance their comfort. On the Glacier Express, the journey begins from St. Mortiz, passing through Chur, Desentis, Brig, and Visp to reach its final destination at Zermatt. At Oberalp pass, it travels at the highest altitude of 2033 meters.

It crosses through 91 tunnels and 291 bridges, including the Gotthard Pass. Travelers are able to enjoy landscape littered with lush meadows, deep gorges, and tall mountains like The Matterhorn, The Dom, and Piz Bernina. The Rhaetian Railway in the Albula/Bernina landscape has been earmarked by UNESCO as a world heritage site, and the landscape remains pristine and untouched by any changes.

The 7½-hour journey is made memorable by the restaurant service, which offers 3-course meals, and the Panorama cars in which travelers can enjoy the scenic beauty around them. In addition, travelers are able to obtain different kinds of souvenirs and gift coupons aboard the Glacier Express.

# The Western Highland Railway

One of the most renowned railways in Scotland is the Western Highland railway, which travels from Glasgow to Oban, Fort William, and Malliag. The Gaelic term for the railway, Iron Road to the Isles, is very apt because it describes the awe-inspiring experiences of the passengers on the train that have the privilege of exploring some of the world's most beautiful, natural land-scapes. The train basically has two routes: one portion heads off to Oban and the other stops at Malliag; the former takes 3 hours while in the latter the total traveling time is 5½ hours.

At Glasgow, travelers can enjoy the architecture and culture of Scotland, while both Oban and Malliag are ports. At Fort William, hikers can backpack to Britain's tallest mountain, Ben Nevis. The train provides a spectacular view of places like River Clyde, Loch Lomond, Kilchurn Castle, River Awe, and Achhallder Castle, as well as the wild Rannoch Moor with its old forests, streams, and boulders.

It also passes through a number of scenic bridges, including the famous Glenfinnan

Viaduct, better known by its appearance in the Harry Potter movies as the path for the Hogwarts Express.

After this, passengers can enjoy a view of the islands of Rum and Eigg and the Loch Morar. At the port of Mallaig, the travelers can take in various kinds of marine life, and at Fort William, the Western Highland Museum, Neptune Staircase, and Ben Nevis Distillery are some unmissable locations. In essence, the Western Highland Railway provides an unforgettable experience for the traveler, dotted with numerous ethereal lochs and meadows.

# The Caldervale Line

The Caldervale Line runs through Northern England to connect several important cities of this region. The railway primarily functions to cater to travelers in the localities of West Yorkshire, Greater Manchester, Lancashire, Leeds, North West England, Yorkshire, and the Humber. The train travels between Leeds and Manchester and also connects cities like Bradford, Halifax, Todmorden, Hebden Bridge, Blackburn, Burnley, Preston, and Blackpool.

The Caldervale Line is famously known as an important historic railway in England. From Manchester, it travels via Mills Hills and Castelon to reach Rochdale, which is famous for its museums. Then it proceeds to the Sowerby Bridge. It allows travelers to explore urban and natural locations in England. They can stop at the Smithy Bridge to view Hollingworth Lake and the park surrounding it, as well as the Rochdale Canal, Littleborough, and the Rossendale Fells.

It offers unparalleled access to the wild-hooded beauty of the Pennine Moors. En route, Walsden is popular for the Summit Tunnel and the highest canal lock, as well as its fish and chips delicacy. Hebden Bridge is known for shopping and its Stubbing Wharf Cruises, while Mytholmroyd is a beautiful place for long walks. The Tuel Lane Lock at the Sowerby Bridge and Yorkshire Mill at Dewbury are also very popular among tourists.

At Hailfax, travelers can visit interactive museums, and at Bradford, there is an Industrial Museum. Similarly, at the final destination, Leeds, performances are presented at the Royal Armouries, West Yorkshire Playhouse, and several opera houses.

# The Bergen Line

This is a Norwegian railway, which connects Bergen and Hønefoss. It is rightly known as one of the most beautiful train rides in the world, because it offers the travelers a memorable experience. Aboard this train, passengers get to admire the beautiful vistas of Northern Europe. It is also the highest mainline railway of this region. It links the two most important cities of the country and is probably the only viable means of traveling through the mountains, in winter especially.

The train allows people to gaze at the white snowy beauty around them in a safe and reliable manner. The railway is constructed in harsh terrain and the journey takes about 6½ hours, passing through 39 stations at different places. The typical train ride atop the Bergan railway offers the passenger a scene of fast-flowing, beautiful rivers and rising, formidable mountains. It also crosses the Hardangervidda Plateau at 1,237 meters, while the Finse Station is the highest station on the journey at an elevation of 1,222.2 meters.

The 372 kilometers long railway travels through 182 handcarved tunnels. The railway is also popular for serving those who want to stop at the ski resorts on the journey and those who would like to explore the region of ravines and waterfalls on the Flam Railway, which is one of the steepest railways in the world.

## The Bernina Express

The Bernina Express is a train famous for its panoramic views and splendid sights of the gigantic and impressive Alps. It seamlessly links Northern and Southern Europe because it runs from Chur in Switzerland to Tirano in Italy. It presents an eclectic journey across beautiful locales and passes through the World Heritage Site in the Albula/Bernina Landscapes, called the Rhaetian Railway.

The route derives it beauty from the difference in the landscapes of Switzerland and Italy. The former has a northern, cold climate, while Italy is famous for its sunny warmth. It passes from the Engadine, Bernina Hospiz (2253 metres) through the Poschiavo Valley into Valtellina in Italy. The travelers are able to enjoy a vast variety of scenes, such as the Landwasser viaduct at 65 meters, Schyn Gorge, Morteratsch Glacier, and Brusio spiral viaduct.

Amidst the snowy surroundings, this crimson train renders untouched landscapes accessible for the passengers. It also traverses some of the highest altitudes. The picturesque landscape of Italy, with its palm-lined lakes, provides a sharp contrast to the Swiss glaciers in just 4 hours aboard the Bernina Express. The train ride can be enjoyed with a selection of snacks and drinks, provided in your seat since there is no specific dinning car available.

Bernina Express crosses 196 bridges and 55 tunnels, while the highest point on this journey is at the Bernina Pass, which is 2,253 meters high. The trip is made memorable with bilingual narrations to help tourists enjoy the scenic beauty around them.

# Cinque Terre

This Italian railway connects Levanto and La Spezia. Cinque Terre is a beautiful region, which consists of five villages: Riomaggiore, Manarola, Corniglia, Vernazza, and Monterosso. For its scenic beauty, unique location, and historic importance, UNESCO has listed this region as a World Heritage Site. The locality is popular for its trails, on which people can hike or walk to enjoy the rich cultural vibe of this region.

Surprisingly enough, it can be accessed by a train system. Compared to walking, the train provides a feasible option for people who want to enjoy the views in sufficient time. The Cinque Terre train line has six stops in total from La Spezia to the five main cities mentioned earlier. The time taken to travel from La Spezia to the five cities is between 5-10 minutes and with this fairly quick journey, tourists and visitors can easily resume walking and explore locations at their leisure.

The train runs every hour, but its timings could be sporadic and have to be verified beforehand. The easiest way to reach this beautiful site is to take the Cinque Terre train from Milan to Levanto, from Genoa to Levanto, or from Levanto to Monterosso. The station at La Spezia also connects to Monterosso, Pisa, and Rome. Each of these routes varies in terms of the time of the journey. The major attraction of this region is its rugged landscape, with steep cliffs perched on the coastline.

## Central Rhine Railway

This train runs in Germany and connects the two beautiful cities of Bingen and Koblenz. The train runs alongside the meandering river of Rhine. The vista presented from the window is breathtaking and stunning. Lush, green valleys adorn the sides, whilst high, unassailable mountains rise in the backdrop during the journey.

The entire travel is likened to a supernal, romantic experience, like something out of a fairy tale. The hills are jagged and uneven, and the fields of German wine leave the passengers awestruck by the greenery. The landscape of this region has been described as dramatic at best, and the ride on this train is obligatory for anyone who wishes to explore the natural beauty of Germany.

The region this train travels through is basically known for producing wine, so travelers get to view well-endowed vineyards on one side and a fast running river on the other. In addition, one can view the scenic fortress of Ehrenbreitstein in Koblenz, as well as several old castles like the castles of Marksburg, Stahleck, Katz, and Maus or the Pfalz castle, which is on an island in the riverbed.

The journey is primarily famous because it allows travelers easily to see some of the most important historic sites of Germany, such as its melancholic stone and brick castles set against the emerald hills. Aboard the train, the passengers are provided with a range of services for entertainment and relaxation.

# Semmering Railway

The Semmering Railway is a European train that runs in Austria and connects the areas of Gloggnitz, leading to Semmering and stopping at its destination in Mürzzuschlag. The historical background of its construction and architectural conception in the mid-1800s is fascinating because the railway was built in a rugged terrain, at high altitude. The Semmering railway has 14 tunnels, 16 viaducts, 100 stone bridges, and 10 iron bridges.

The massive amount of effort and technical innovation the construction of this railway led to was mindboggling. The unique amalgamation of technology with the natural scenic embellishments of high mountains and deep valleys made the Semmery Railway a riveting journey for passengers.

UNESCO labeled this railway a World Heritage site due to its historic significance, which helps to perserve the original surroundings. The train passes through a volley of rich and thick forests and deep, green meadows. The Semmering Railway became important because it allows people to access this beautiful region easily and inhabit it by building houses and hotels to promote tourism. The villas built en route are also a remnant of Gothic and Renaissance architecture.

Perhaps the most fascinating aspect of its construction is that it was built over a high gradient and special locomotives had to be developed to maneuver the sharp curvature of the turns. Aboard the train, the passengers are provided a number of indispensable services for eating, relaxing, and entertainment. The stations at which the Semmering train stops also have exhibitions to cater to the travelers.

# Trans–Siberian Railway

The Trans-Siberian proper railway runs from Moscow to Vladivostok and is a part of the larger network of the Trans-Siberian Railway, which includes the Trans-Mongolian route and Trans-Manchurian route. The first part of it was built to connect the Russian cities of Moscow and Vladivostok. The railway stretches over 9,000 kilometers and guided tours across the region take about 13 days. The entire Trans-Siberian Railway, including three of these aforementioned routes, is the largest railway line in the world.

The journey atop the Trans-Siberian is singularly enthralling and memorable because the train traverses two distinctive continents and weaves its way through different time zones, leaving the passengers amazed. The travelers can explore many scenic locations on the path, such as the Ekaterinburg in the Ural Mountains, Irkutsk (the capital of Eastern Siberia), and the spectacular and naturally wonderful Lake Baikal, the world's deepest freshwater lake. Moscow as the starting point is amazing with its Red Square, St. Basil's Cathedral, and Armory Chamber.

The stop at Irkutsk is known as the Paris of Siberia, because of its combination of modern and ancient buildings and bridges across Angara River. The Limnological Museum and Museum of Wooden Architecture are the famous places in this region. The train passes through Ulan Ude as well, which is an unusual, historic city with a large Buddhist population and ethnographic museum, after which the passengers can head to Vladivostok.

# The Hundred Valley Railway

This railway is better known as the Centovalli Railway. It is designed to be an excursion train to specifically cater to the sightseeing and touring needs of visitors. The railway is famous for passing through a hundred picturesque valleys. The railway is designed to link the Gotthard and Simplon lines and Ticino and Valais in the shortest distance. Traveling over a distance of 60 kilometers, the passengers are presented with scenes which meld from high mountains, deep gorges, and slushing waterfalls into lush forests. Through high viaducts, several tunnels, and sharp turns, it connects Domodossola in Italy to Locarno in Switzerland.

Between Masera and Santa Maria Maggiore in Italy and Verdasio and Intragna in Switzerland, the gradient shifts sharply and the train travels through steep terrain. Overall, it takes around 2 hours to reach one's destination on this train. The beauty of the landscape makes a trip on Centovalli compulsory for the globetrotter, since it also has about 22 stations where one can stop and admire the surrounding areas.

The train itself has an old-fashioned interior which makes the journey more like a trip down the memory lane, albeit one with a splendid landscape. Other than the hundred different valleys, a traveler is able to see the wild Melezza River from the train, lined with large rocks and sturdy, green trees. The Panoramic Express allows travelers to view the region easily, since it travels at a slower speed.

# Section 3 – Directory of Train Stations

## Train Stations in Austria

### Vienna

Wien Hauptbahnhof

Am Hauptbahnhof 1100

Vienna, Austria

Phone: +43 (0)5-1717


### Wien Westbahnhof

Europaplatz 2, 1150

Vienna, Austria

Phone: +43 5 1717


### Bahnhof Floridsdorf

Franz-Jonas-Platz, A-1210

Vienna, Austria

Phone: +431580031010


### Franz-Josefs-Bahnhof

Julius-Tandler-Platz 3, 1090

Vienna, Austria

Phone: +431580031020


**City Airport Train**

P.O.Box 11300 Wien-Flughafen

Vienna, Austria

Phone: **+43 1 25 250**


**Bahnhof Wien Nord**

Praterstem, 1020

Vienna, Austria

Phone: +4351717


**Bahnhof Wien Mitte**

Gigergasse 1030

Vienna, Austria

Phone: + 431580031070


**Bahnhof Liesing**

LiesingerPlatz-1, 1230

Vienna, Austria

Phone: +4318692615

**Bahnhof Meidling**

Eichenstrashe 1120

Vienna, Austria

Phone: +4351717

**Bahnhof Wien Hutteldorf**

Keisslergasse 1, Wien 1140

Vienna, Austria

Phone: +4351717

**Bahnhof Nussdorf**

Heiligenstadter Strashe Wien 1190

Vienna, Austria

**Hauptbahnhof Wien**

Südtiroler Platz, Wien, Österreich

Vienna, Austria

**Linz**

Reisebüro am Bahnhof

Bahnhofplatzn3-6, 4020

Linz, Austria

Phone: +43 732 930003170

## Linz Hauptbahnhof

Bahnhofplatz, 4020

Linz, Austria

Phone: +43 (0) 5-1717

## Graz

Hauptbahnhof Graz

Europaplatz 4

Graz, Austria

Phone: +43 51717

## Graz-feld.flughafen

Betrieb GmbH Feldkirchen,

Steiermark A-8073

Graz, Austria

## Salzburg

Salzburg Hauptbahnhof

Südtiroler Platz 1

5020 Salzburg

Phone: +43662 93000

## Innsbruck

Innsbruck Hauptbahnhof

Südtiroler Platz 7

A-6020 Innsbruck

Austria

Phone: +43 51717

## Klagenfurt

Klagenfurt Hauptbahnhof

Walter-von-der-Vogelweideplatz, 9020

Klagenfurt, Austria

Phone: +43 (0)5-1717

## Villach

Villach Hauptbahnhof

Bahnhofplatz, 9500

Villach, Austria

Phone: +43 (0) 5-1717

## St.Polten

St. Pölten Hauptbahnhof

Bahnhofplatz, 3100

St. Pölten, Austria
Phone: +43 2742 93000-0

# Train Stations in Upper Austria

Most railway stations in Upper Austria are quite small. They operate lines that run to other closeby villages and small towns. Unlike other urban stations, these railway hubs are not multiple stories with a lot of facilities and services.

## Wels

Wels Hauptbahnhof

Bahnhofstraße, 4600

Wels, Austria

## Attnang-Puchheim

Attnang-Puchheim Station

Rennerplatz 6,4800

Attnang-Puchheim

Austria

## Neukirchen an der Vöckla

Neukirchen-Gampern Station

4851 Gampern

Austria

## Zipf

Redl-Zipf Railway Station

Langwies 16

4871 Zipf

Austria

## Timelkam

Timelkam Station

Leidern 17

4850 Timelkam

Austria

## Vöcklabruck

Vöcklabruck Station

Bahnhofstrasse 17, 4840

Vöcklabruck

Austria

# Train Stations in Brussels

**Brussels Midi (South) Station**

Av Fonsny 47B, 1060

Brussels, Belgium

**Brussels Central Station**

1000 Brussels, Belgium

**Brussels Nord (North) Station**

76 rue du Progrès, 1030

Schaerbeek, Brussels, Belgium

**Berchem-Sainte-Agathe Railway Station**

1082 Berchem-Sainte-Agathe

Brussels, Belgium

**Bockstael Railway Station**

Laeken, 1020

Brussels, Belgium

**Schuman Station**

Rue de la Loi/Wetstraat

1040 Brussels, Belgium

**Brussels-Luxembourg Railway Station**

Trierstraat / Rue du Trèves, 1000

Brussels, Belgium

Phone: +32 2 528 28 28

# Train Stations in Czech Republic

## Brno

Brno hlavní nádraží (Brno Main Railway Station)

Nádražní 418/1, 602 00

Brno, Czech Republic

Phone: +420 972 624 552, +420 972 625 430

## Pardubice

Pardubice hlavní nádraží (Pardubice Main Railway Station)

Jana Pernera 217, 530 02

Pardubice, Czech Republic

## Prague

Praha hlavní nádraží (Prague Main Railway Station)

Wilsonova 300/8, 110 00

Prague, Czech Republic

Phone: +420 224 214 886, +420 224 217 948

**Praha-Holešovice Railway Station**

Partyzánská 1546/26, 17000

Prague, Czech Republic


**Praha Masarykovo nádraží**

Havlíčkova 1014/2, 110 00

Prague, Czech Republic


**Praha-Čakovice Railway Station**

K přejezdu, 196 00

Prague, Czech Republic


**Praha-Libeň Railway Station**

Českomoravská 316/24, 190 00

Prague, Czech Republic


**Praha-Smíchov Railway Station**

Nádražní, 150 00

Prague, Czech Republic

Phone: + 420 224 617 686

# Train Stations in Denmark

## Copenhagen

Copenhagen Airport, Kastrup Station

Lufthavns Boulevarden 6,

2770 Kastrup

Copenhagen, Denmark

Phone: +45 32 31 32 31


## Copenhagen Central Station

Banegardspladsen 7, Vestebro

Copenhagen, Denmark

Phone:  +45 33 14 04 00


## Avedøre Train Station

52 Kærgårdsvej, Hvidovre

Copenhagen, Denmark


## Emdrup Station

Tuborgvej 170

2400 København NV

Copenhagen, Denmark

Phone: +45 70 13 14 15

**Skovlunde Train Station**

4 Skovlunde Torv, Skovlunde

Copenhagen, Denmark

Phone: +45 33 14 17 01

**Nordhavn Station**

Østbanegade 120

2100 København Ø

Denmark

**Svanemøllen Station**

Strandvejen 59

2100 København

Copenhagen, Denmark

**Hellerup Station**

Ryvangs Alle 79 C

2900 Hellerup

Copenhagen, Denmark

**Bagsværd Train Station**

142 Bagsværd Hovedgade

Copenhagen, Denmark

## Valby Train Station

1A Mellemtoftevej, Valby

Copenhagen, Denmark

## Flintholm Train Station

Flintholm Allé 55

2000 Frederiksberg

Copenhagen, Denmark

## Farum Train Station

1 Jernbanevej, Farum,

Furesø Kommune

Copenhagen, Denmark

## Sindal

Sindal Station

Jernbanegade 8 DK-9870

Sindal, Denmark

Phone: +45 98 93 66 93

## Frederikshavn

Frederikshavn Train Station

Havnepladsen 30, DK-9990

Frederikshavn, Denmark

**Aalbæk**

Aalbæk Train Station

Stationsvej 21, DK-9982

Ålbæk, Denmark

**Aalborg**

Aalborg Train Station

John. F Kennedys Plads3, 9000

Aalborg, Denmark

**Aarhus**

Aarhus Central Station

Banegårdspladsen 1, 8000

Aarhus, Denmark

Phone: +45 70 13 14 15

# Train Stations in Estonia

**Tartu**

Tartu Railway Station

Vaksali 6, 50409

Tartu, Estonia

**Tallinn**

(Balti Jaam) Baltic Train Station

Toompuiestee 37, 10133

Tallinn, Estonia

# Train Stations in Finland

**Helsinki**

Helsinki Central Railway Station (Helsingin päärautatieasema)

Asema-aukio, 00100

Helsinki, Finland

Phone: +358 600 41902

**Lathi**

Lathi Railway Station

Mannerheiminkatu 15, 15100

Lahti, Finland

Phone: 0600 41 900

**Ostrobothnia**

Bennäs Railway Station

Stationsvägen 9,68910

Bennäs, Finland

**Kokkola Railway Station**

Rautatienkatu 1, 67100

Kokkola, Finland

Phone: 0600 41 900

## Oulainen Railway Station

Rautatienkatu 8, 83600

Oulainen, Finland

## Ylivieska Railway Station

Asemakatu 11, 84100

Ylivieska, Finland

## Oulu

Oulu Railway Station

Rautatienkatu 11A, 90100

Oulu, Finland

## Kempele Railway Station

Rautiontie 27, 90440

Kempele, Finland

## Lappeenranta

Lappeenranta Railway Station

Ratakatu 23, 53100

Lappeenranta, Finland

## Iisalmi

Iisalmi Railway Station

Savonkatu 32, 74100

Iisalmi, Finland

## Joensuu

Joensuu Railway Station

Itäranta 12, 80100

Joensuu, Finland

## Jyväskylä

Jyväskylä Railway Station

Hannikaisenkatu 20, 40100

Jyväskylä, Finland

## Kajaani

Kajaani Railway Station

Asema-alue 87100

Kajaani,Finland

Phone: 0600 41 902

## Kouvola

Kouvola Railway Station

Hallituskatu 3 45100

Kouvola, Finland

Phone: +600 41 902

## Pieksämäki

Pieksämäki Railway Station

Asemakatu 2, 76100

Pieksämäki, Finland

## Pori

Pori Railway Station

Asema-aukio 3, 28100

Pori, Finland

## Seinäjoki

Seinäjoki Railway Station

Valtionkatu 1, 60100

Seinäjoki, Finland

Phone: +600 41 900

## Varkaus

Varkaus Railway Station

Relanderinkatu 18, 78200

Varkaus, Finland

# Train Stations in France

## Gare de Strasbourg

20 Place de la gare, 67000

Strasbourg, France

Phone: +333 88 32 51 49


## Mulhouse Ville Train Station

10 Avenue du Général-Leclerc, 68100

Mulhouse, France


## Agen Train Station

1 place Rabelais, 47000

Agen, France

Phone: 05 53 77 81 03


## Gare de Bayonne

Place Pereire, 64100

Bayonne, France

Phone: 05 59 50 84 93


## Gare de Biarritz

Allée du Moura, 64200

Biarritz, France

Phone: 05 59 50 83 08

**Gare de Bordeaux-Saint-Jean**

33800 Bordeaux, France

Phone: 05 56 34 50 50

**Gare de Dax**

Avenue de la gare, 40100

Dax, France

Phone: 05 58 58 76 69

**Gar de Hendaye**

Boulevard G,n,ral De Gaulle, 64700

Hendaye , France

Phone: 05 59 48 85 65

**Paris-Gare de Lyon**

20 boulevard Diderot 75012

Paris, France

Phone: +33 (0)8 90 64 06 50

## Paris-Gare du Nord

18 Rue Dunkerque 75010, 112,
rue de Maubeuge 75010
Paris, France
Phone: +33 890 640 650

## Paris-Gare de l'Est

Place du 11 novembre 1918 75010
Paris, France
Phone: +33 (0)8 90 64 06 50

## Paris-Gare Montparnasse

17, boulevard Vaugirard4
Paris, France
Phone: 01/40481424

## Paris-Gare d'Austerlitz

55, quai d'Austerlitz 85 quai d'Austerlitz
75013
Paris, France
Phone: 01/53601284

## Paris Charles de Gaulle Train Station

BP 35042 Tremblay 95716 Roissy CDG
cedex

Paris, France

Phone: 01/48796139

## Gare de Bercy

48 bis boulevard de Bercy 75012

Paris, France

Phone: +33 (0)8 90 64 06 50

## Gare de Metz-Ville

1, place du Général de Gaulle, 570000

Metz, France

## Nancy Ville Train Station

3 place Thiers 54000

Nancy, France

Phone: 33 (0)3 83 35 22 41

## Gare Lorraine TGV

57420 Louvigny,

Lorraine, France

## Le Havre Graville Train Station

12 Rue de Magellan, 76600

Le Havre, France

Phone: 02 32 92 95 63

## Rouen-Rive-Droite

Place Bernard Tissot

Saint-etienne-du-Rouvray, 76000

France

Phone: 02 35 52 12 63

## Gare de Caen

15, Place de la gare, 14000

Caen, France

Phone: 33 (0)2 31 27 14 14

## Gare d'Amiens

47, place Alphonse Fiquet, 80000

Amiens, France

Phone: 03 22 82 14 33

## Château-Thierry Railway Station

Place Jean Monnet, 2400

Château Thierry France
Phone: 33 (0)3 23 83 51 14

**Gare de Creil**
Place Charles De Gaulle, 60100
Creil, France
Phone: 03 44 65 71 07

**Gare de Saint-Quentin**
Place André Baudez, 02100
Saint-Quentin, France

**Gare d-Angers-Saint-Laud**
1 esplanade de la gare 49100
Angers, France

**Le Mans Train Station**
Place du 8 mai 1945, 72000
Le Mans, France
Phone: 02 43 21 73 41

**Gare de Nantes**
27, boulevard de Stalingrad

BP 34112

44041 Nantes cedex 1

Nantes, France

## Gare de Brest

8, Place du 19Šme RI, 29200

Brest, France

Phone: 02 29 00 51 63

## Lorient Train Station

rue Beauvais, 56100

Lorient, France

Phone:  02 97 88 42 65

## Gare de Quimper

Place Louis Armand, 29000

Quimper, France

## Gare de Redon

Place Michel Mac,35600

Redon, France

Phone: 02 99 71 74 12

## Gare de Rennes

Place de la Gare, 35000
Rennes, France

# Train Stations in Germany

**Freiburg Hauptbahnhof**

Bismarckallee, 79098

Freiburg, Germany

Phone: +49 761 2121055


**Karlsruhe Hauptbahnhof**

Bahnhofsplatz 1

Karlsruhe, Germany

Phone: +49 721 9381055


**Mannheim Hauptbahnhof**

Willy-Brandt-Platz 17, 68161

Mannheim, Germany

Phone: +49 621 40049-0


**Stuttgart Hauptbahnhof**

Arnulf-Klett-Platz, 70173

Stuttgart, Germany

Phone: +4971120921055


**Ulm Hauptbahnhof**

Friedrich-Ebert-Str. 11, 89073
Ulm, Germany
Phone: +49 731 1021055

**Augsburg Hauptbahnhof**
Viktoriastr. 1, 86150
Augsburg, Germany
Phone: +49 89 13081055

**Bayreuth Hauptbahnhof**
Bahnhofstr. 20, 95444
Bayreuth, Germany
Phone: +49 180 5996633

**Fürth (Bayern) Hauptbahnhof**
Bahnhofplatz 1, 90762
Fürth, Germany

**Ingolstadt Hauptbahnhof**
Bahnhofstraße 885051
Ingolstadt, Germany
Phone: +49 180 5 512 512

## München Hauptbahnhof

Bayerstr. 10a, 80335

Munich, Germany

Phone: +498913081055

## München Ost

Orleansplatz 11, 81667

München, Germany

## München-Pasing

Pasinger Bahnhofs platz 9, 81241

Munich, Germany

## Nürnberg Hauptbahnhof

Bahnhofsplatz 1, 90402

Nürnberg, Germany

Phone: 0911 2401342

## Passau Hauptbahnhof

Bahnhofstraße 29, 94032

Passau, Germany

## Regensburg Hauptbahnhof

Bahnhofstr. 18, 93047
Regensburg, Germany
Phone: +49 180 5252525

**Rosenheim Bahnhof**
Bahnhofstr. 1
83022 Rosenheim
Germany

**Würzburg Hauptbahnhof**
Bahnhofplatz 4
97070 Würzburg
Phone: 0180 5252525

**Berlin Hauptbahnhof**
Europaplatz 1, D-10551
Berlin, Germany
Phone: +49302971055

**Berlin Ostbahnhof**
Koppenstr. 3 10243
Berlin, Germany
Phone: 01805 99 66 33

**Berlin Südkreuz**

General-Pape-Straße 1, 12101

Berlin, Germany

Phone: +49 180 6 252525


**Berlin Zoologischer Garten Railway Station**

Hardenbergplatz, 10623

Berlin, Germany

# Train Stations in Hungary

**Budapest**

**Keleti Railway Station**
Kerepesi út 2/6,
District VIII, 1087
Budapest, Hungary
Phone: +36 1 413 4610

**Nyugati Railway Station**
Teréz körút 55/57,
District VI, 1062
Budapest, Hungary
Phone: +36 1 349 8503

**Déli Railway Station**
Krisztina körút 37/A,
I kerület, 1013
Budapest, Hungary
Phone: +36 1 375 6593

**Kelenföld Railway Station**

Etele tér 5/7, 1115

Budapest, Hungary

Phone: +36 1 203 3238

## Debrecen

## Central Station of Debrecen

12 Petőfi Square, 4025

Debrece, Hungary

Phone: +36 52 346 316

## Vasúti megállóhely

Csapókert, 4033

Debrecen, Hungary

## Miskloc

## Tiszai Railway Station

Kandó Kálmán tér 1-3,3527

Miskloc, Hungary

Phone: +36 40 494 494

## Szeged

**Vasútállomás Railway Station**

Indítóház tér, 6725

Szege, Hungary

Phone: +36 62 426 821

**Dunaújváros**

**Dunaújváros vasútállomás**

Kandó Kálmán tér 1, 2400

Dunaújváros, Hungary

Phone: +36 25 436 987

**Pusztaszabolcs vasútállomás**

Sport utca 13, 2490

Pusztaszabolcs, Hungary

**Vasútállomás**

8000 Székesfehérvár, Hungary

Phone: +36 22 313 060

**Kiskunfélegyháza**

MÁV Magyar Államvasutak

Kossuth Lajos út 37, 6100
Kiskunfélegyháza, Hungary
Phone: +36 40 494 494

## MÁV Dabasi Állomásfőnökség
Vonat utca 5, 2370
Dabas, Hungary
Phone: +36 29 360 114

## Pécsi Vasútállomás
7623 Pécs, Hungary

## Sásd Vasútállomás
Rákóczi Ferenc utca 36
7370 Sásd, Hungary

## Győr Vasútállomás
Révai Miklós utca 2-4
9021 Győr, Hungary

## Győrszentiván
9011 Győr, Hungary

**MÁV Magyar Államvasutak**
Béke tér 2, 8500
Pápa, Hungary
Phone: +36 1 444 4499

**Nyíregyháza külső**
4400 Nyíregyháza, Hungary

**Sóstó**
4400 Nyíregyháza, Hungary

**Kecskemét Train Station**
Kecskemét, Hungary
Székesfehérvár

**MÁV Magyar Államvasutak Zrt.**
Béke tér 5-7, 8000
Székesfehérvár, Hungary
Phone: +36 40 494 494

# Train Stations in Ireland

## Ashtown Railway Station

Ashtown Road

Dublin, Ireland

Phone: +353 (0) 1 888 0043


## Adamstown Railway Station

R120 Adamstown

Co. South Dublin, Ireland

Phone: +353 (0) 1 828 1060


## Balbriggan Railway Station

Station Rd., Balbriggan

Co. Dublin, Ireland

Phone: +353 (0) 1 828 1360


## Donabate Railway Station

Turvey Rd., Donabate

Co. Dublin, Ireland

Phone: +353 (0) 1 843 6082


## Blackrock Railway Station

Bath Place, Blackrock
Co. Dublin, Ireland
Phone: +353 (0) 1 88 80187

**Dalkey Railway Station**
Ardeveehan Rd., Dalkey
Co. Dublin, Ireland
Phone: +353 (0) 1 828 6240

**Dún Laoghaire Mallin Railway Station**
Crofton Rd., Dún Laoghaire
Co. Dublin, Ireland
Phone: +353 (0) 1 828 6180

**Booterstown Railway Station**
Rock Rd., Blackrock
Co. Dublin, Ireland
Phone: +353 (0) 1 88 0186

**Glenageary D.A.R.T. Station**
Station Rd., Glenageary
Co. Dublin, Ireland
Phone: +353 (0) 1 828 6220

**Sandycove & Glasthule D.A.R.T. Station**

Summerhill Rd., Dún Laoghaire

Co. Dublin, Ireland

Phone: +353 1 828 6200

**Salthill & Monsktown D.A.R.T. Station**

Dún Laoghaire

Co. Dublin, Ireland

Phone: +353 (0) 828 6160

**Killiney Railway Station**

Iarnród Éireann

Station Rd., Killiney

Co. Dublin, Ireland

Phone: +353 (0) 1 828 6260

**Portmarnock Railway Station**

Iarnród Éireann

Station Rd., Portmarnock

Co. Dublin, Ireland

Phone: +353 1 888 0100

## Park West & Cherry Orchard Railway Station

Irish Rail, Cherry Orchard Avenue
Dublin
Co. Dublin, Ireland
Phone: +353 1 828 1000

## Rusk & Lusk Train Station

Station Rd., Lusk
Co. Dublin, Ireland
Phone: +353 1 8437261

## Malahide Railway Station

Iarnród Éireann, Malahide
Co. Dublin, Ireland
Phone: +353 (0) 1 828 6960

## Seapoint D.A.R.T. Station

Blackrock, Dublin
Co. Dublin, Ireland
Phone: +353 1 828 6140

## Skerries Train Station

Station Rd., Skerries

Co. Dublin, Ireland

Phone: +353 1 849 1223

## Shankill Railway Station

Iarnród Éireann

Shanganagh, Shankill

Co. Dublin, Ireland

Phone: +353 1 828 6280

## Dublin Connolly Railway Station

Ameins Street

Dublin 1, Ireland

Phone: +353 (0) 1 703 2358-9

## Docklands Railway Station

Upper Sheriff Street, Dockland

Dublin 1, Ireland

Phone: +353 (0) 1 828 6380

## Pearse Railway Station

Westland Row, R118

Dublin 2, Ireland

Phone: +353 (0) 1 703 3633

## Grand Canal Dock Railway Station
Barrow Street
Dublin 2, Ireland
Phone: +353 (0) 1 703 1470

## Tara Street Station
George's Quay, R802
Dublin 2, Ireland
Phone: +353 1 7032596

## Clontarf Railway Station
Clontarf Rd., Clontarf
Dublin 3, Ireland
Phone: +353 (0) 1 828 6440

## Killester D.A.R.T. Station
Killester
Dublin 3, Ireland
Phone: +353 (0) 1 828 6460

## Lansdowne Railway Station

Lansdowne Rd.

Dublin 4, Ireland

Phone: +353 (0) 1 888 0183

**Sydney Parade Railway Station**

Sydney Parade Ave.

Dublin 4, Ireland

Phone: +353 1 888 0185

**Sandymount Railway Station**

Sandymount Ave., Sandymount

Dublin 4, Ireland

Phone: +353 1 888 0184

**Harmonstown Railway Station**

Iarnród Éireann

Harmonstown Rd., Harmonstown

Dublin 5, Ireland

Phone: +353 (0) 1 828 6480

**Kilbarrack D.A.R.T. Station**

Bryefield Rd., Kilbarrack

Dublin 5, Ireland

Phone: +353 (0) 1 828 6820

## Raheny D.A.R.T. Station

Raheny

Dublin 5, Ireland

Phone: +353 1 828 6800

## Broombridge Railway Station

Broombridge, Cabra

Dublin 7, Ireland

Phone: +353 (0) 1 836 6222

## Heuston Railway Station

St. John Rd. West

Dublin 8, Ireland

Phone: +353 (0) 1 703 2132

## Drumcondra Railway Station

Lower Drumcondra Rd., Drumcondra

Dublin 9, Ireland

Phone: +353 (0) 1 830 5311

## Bayside Railway Station

Sutton

Dublin 13, Ireland

Phone: +353 (0) 1 828 6880

## Clongriffin Railway Station

Station Way, Clongriffin

Dublin 13, Ireland

Phone: +353 1 836 6222

## Sutton D.A.R.T. Station

Station Rd., Sutton

Dublin 13, Ireland

Phone: +353 1 828 6900

## Howth D.A.R.T. Station

Howth

Dublin 13, Ireland

Phone: +353 (0) 1 828 6920

## Castleknock Railway Station

Castleknock

Dublin 15, Ireland

Phone: +353 (0) 1 820 1706

## Clonsilla Railway Station

Clonsilla Rd., Clonsilla

Dublin 15, Ireland

Phone: +353 (0) 1 821 1378

## Cooline Railway Station

Carpenterstown Rd., Carpenterstown

Dublin 15, Ireland

Phone: +353 (0) 1 820 1957

## Hansfield Railway Station

Ongar

Dublin 15, Ireland

Phone: +353 (0) 1 828 1540

## Clondalkin Fonthill Railway Station

Fonthill Rd., Clondalkin

Dublin 22, Ireland

Phone: +353 1 836 6222

## Galway (Ceantt) Railway Station

Iarnród Éireann

Station Rd., Galway

Co. Galway, Ireland

Phone: +353 (0) 91 561444

## Ardrahan Railway Station

Ardrahan

Co. Galway, Ireland

Phone: +353 (0) 1 836 6222

## Athenry Railway Station

Church Street, Athenry

Co. Galway, Ireland

Phone: +353 (0) 9 184 4020

## Attymon Railway Station

Attymon, Athenry

Co. Galway, Ireland

Phone: +353 (0) 1 836 6222

## Ballinasloe Railway Station

Station Rd., Ballinasloe

Co. Galway, Ireland

Phone: +353 (0) 9096 42105

## Gort Railway Station

Co. Galway, Ireland

Phone: +353 1 836 6222

## Woodlown Train Station

Iarnród Éireann, R359

Woodlawn, Ballinasloe

Co. Galway, Ireland

Phone: +353 1 836 6222

## Kildare County

## Kildare Railway Station

Iarnród Éireann

Station Rd., Kildare

Co. Kildare, Ireland

Phone: +353 (0) 45 521224

## Athy Railway Station

Church Rd., Athy

Co. Kildare, Ireland

Phone: +353 (0) 5 073 1966

## Hazelhatch & Celbridge Railway Station

Iarnród Éireann

Hazelhatch Rd., Celbridge

Co. Kildare, Ireland

Phone: +353 (0) 828 1080


## Kilcock Railway Station

Iarnród Éireann

Co. Kildare, Ireland

Phone: +353 1 836 6222


## Lexilip Confey Station

Iarnród Éireann

Captain's Hill, Lexilip

Co. Kildare, Ireland

Phone: +353 (0) 1 888 0055


## Louisa Bridge Station

Iarnród Éireann, Lexilip

Co. Kildare, Ireland

Phone: +353 (0) 1 888 0056

## Sallins & Naas Railway Station

Iarnród Éireann, Sallins

Co. Kildare, Ireland

Phone: +353 1 836 6222

## Maynooth Railway Station

Iarnród Éireann, Maynooth

Co. Kildare, Ireland

Phone: +353 1 6285509

## Monasterevin Railway Station

Canal Harbour, Monasterevin

Co. Kildare, Ireland

Phone: +353 (0) 45 527419

## Newbrige Railway Station

Iarnród Éireann

Station Rd., Newbridge

Co. Kildare, Ireland

Phone: +353 (0) 45 431219

## Kilkenny County

## MacDonagh Railway Station

Iarnród Éireann

Carlow Rd., Kilkenny

Co. Kilkenny, Ireland

Phone: +353 (0) 56 772 2024

## Thomastown Railway Station

Iarnród Éireann

Station Rd., Thomastown

Co. Kilkenny, Ireland

Phone: +353 56 772 4218

## Clare County

## Ennis Railway Station

Quinn Rd., Ennis

Co. Clare, Ireland

Phone: +353 (0) 65 684 0444

## Sixmilebridge Railway Station

R471, Sixmilebridge

Co. Clare, Ireland

Phone: +353 1 836 6222

## Cork County

## Kent Railway Station

Lower Glanmire Rd., Cork City

Co. Cork, Ireland

Phone: +353 (0) 21 450 6766

## Banteer Railway Station

Banteer

Co. Cork, Ireland

Phone: +353 (0) 29 56004

## Carrigaloe Railway Station

Carrigaloe, Cobh

Co. Cork, Ireland

Phone: +353 1 836 6222

## Cobh Railway Station

Cobh

Co. Cork, Ireland

Phone: +353 (0) 21 481 1655

## Rushbrooke Railway Station

Cobh

Co. Cork, Ireland

Phone: +353 1 836 6222

## Carrigtwohill Railway Station

Carrigtwohill

Co. Cork, Ireland

Phone: +353 1 836 6222

## Charleville Railway Station

Railway Rd., Charleville

Co. Cork, Ireland

Phone: +353 (0) 63 81235

## Fota Railway Station

Fota Wildfire Park

Co. Cork, Ireland

Phone: +353 1 836 6222

## Glounthane Railway Station

Iarnród Éireann, Glounthaune

Co. Cork, Ireland

Phone: +353 1 836 6222

## Little Island Railway Station

Co. Cork, Ireland

Phone: +353 1 836 6222

## Mallow Railway Station

Iarnród Éireann

Annabella, Mallow

Co. Cork, Ireland

phone: +353 (0) 22 21120

## Midleton Railway Station

Midleton

Co. Cork, Ireland

Phone: +353 1 836 6222

## Millstreet Railway Station

Iarnród Éireann, Millstreet

Co. Cork, Ireland

phone: +353 (0) 29 70096

## Muine Bheag (Bagenalstown) Railway Station

Iarnród Éireann

Station Rd., Muine Bheag

Co. Carlow, Ireland

Phone: +353 (0) 59 972 1302


## Carlow Railway Station

Railway Rd., Carlow

Co. Carlow, Ireland

Phone: +353 (0) 59 9131633


## Kerry County


## Farranfore Railway Station

Iarnród Éireann, Farranfore

Co. Kerry, Ireland

Phone: +353 (0) 66 976 4101


## Killarney Railway Station

Iarnród Éireann

Fair Hill, Killarney

Co. Kerry, Ireland

Phone: +353 (0) 64 663 1067

## Rathmore Railway Station

Iarnród Éireann, rathmore

Co. Kerry, Ireland

Phone: +353 64 58006

## Casement Railway Station

John Joe Sheehy Rd., Tralee

Co. Kerry, Ireland

Phone: +353 66 712 3522

## Laois County

## Ballybrophy Railway Station

Station Rd., Ballybrophy

Co. Laois, Ireland

Phone: +353 (0) 505 46331

## Portarlington Railway Station

Iarnród Éireann

Station Rd., Portarlington

Co. Laois, Ireland

Phone: +353 5786 23128

## Portlaois Railway Station

Iarnród Éireann

Station Rd., Portlaois

Co. Laois, Ireland

Phone: +353 57 826 1303

Leitrim County

## Carrick-on-Shannon Railway Station

Croghan Rd., Carrick-on-Shannon

Co. Leitrim, Ireland

Phone: +353 (0) 71 9620036

## Dromod Railway Station

Mohill Rd., Dromod

Co. Leitrim, Ireland

Phone: +353 (0) 71 963 8203

## Limerick County

## Castleconnell Railway Station

Railway Rd., Castleconnell

Co. Limerick, Ireland

Phone: +353 1 836 6222

**Colbert Railway Station**

Iarnród Éireann

Parnell Street, Limerick

Co. Limerick, Ireland

Phone: +353 (0) 61 315555

**Longford County**

**Edgeworthstown Railway Station**

Dublin Rd., Edgeworthston

Co. Longford, Ireland

Phone: +353 (0) 43 667 1031

**Longford Railway Station**

Convent Rd., Longford

Co. Longford, Ireland

Phone: +353 (0) 43 334 5208

**Louth County**

## MacBride Railway Station

Dublin Rd., Drogheda

Co. Louth, Ireland

Phone: +353 (0) 41 983 8749

## Dundalk Clarke Railway Station

Carrickmacross Rd., Dundalk

Co. Louth, Ireland

Phone: +353 (0) 87 950 0100

## Mayo County

## Ballina Railway Station

Station Rd., Ballina

Co. Mayo, Ireland

Phone: +353 (0) 96 20229

## Ballyhaunis Railway Station

Ballyhaunis

Co. Mayo, Ireland

Phone: +353 (0) 94 9630009

## Castlebar Railway Station

Station Rd., Castlebar

Co. Mayo, Ireland

Phone: +353 (0) 94 902 1222

## Claremorris Railway Station

Station Rd., Claremorris

Co. Mayo, Ireland

Phone: +353 (0) 94 937 1011

## Foxford Railway Station

Iarnród Éireann, Foxford

Co. Mayo, Ireland

Phone: +353 1 836 6222

## Manulla Junction Station

Co. Mayo, Ireland

Phone: +353 1 836 6222

## Westport Train Station

Iarnród Éireann

Atlamont Street, Westport

Co. Mayo, Ireland

Phone: +353 98 25253

## Meath County

## Dunboyne Railway Station

Dunboyne

Co. Meath, Ireland

Phone: +353 1 836 6222

## Enfield Railway Station

Enfield

Co. Meath, Ireland

Phone: +353 (0) 1 628 5509

## Gromanstown Railway Station

Co. Meath, Ireland

Phone: +353 (0) 1 828 360

## Laytown Railway Station

Laytown

Co. Meath, Ireland

Phone: +353 (0) 41 982 7698

## M3 Parkway Railway Station
Co. meath, Ireland
Phone: +353 1 836 6222

## Offaly County

## Clara Railway Station
Railway Rd., Clara
Co. Offaly, Ireland
Phone: +353 (0) 57 931105

## Tullamore Railway Station
Iarnród Éireann
Kilcruttin, Tullamore
Co.Offaly, Ireland
Phone; +353 57 932 1431

## Roscommon County

## Boyle Railway Station
Station Rd., Boyle
Co. Roscommon, Ireland
Phone: +353 (0) 71 9662027

## Castlerea Railway Station

Church Rd., Castlerea

Co. Roscommon, Ireland

Phone: +353 (0) 94 962 0031

## Roscommon Railway Station

Iarnród Éireann, Abbeytown

Co. Rsocommon, Ireland

Phone: +353 903 26201

## Silgo County

## Ballymote Railway Station

Carrownanty, Ballymote

Co. Silgo, Ireland

Phone: +353 (0) 7191 83311

## Collooney Railway Station

Collooney

Co. Silgo, Ireland

Phone: +353 1 836 6222

## Tipperary County

### Birdhill Railway Station

Birdhill

Co. Tipperary, Ireland

Phone: +353 (0) 61 379118

### Cahir Railway Station

Church Street, Cahir

Co. Tipperary, Ireland

Phone: +353 (0) 1 836 6222

### Carrick-on-Suir Railway Station

Cregg Rd., Carrick-on-Suir

Co. Tipperary, Ireland

Phone: +353 (0) 51 640044

### Clonmel Railway Station

Thomas Street, Clonmel

Co. Tipperay, Ireland

Phone: +353 (0) 52 21982

## Cloughjordan Railway Station

Templemore Rd., Cloughordan

Co. Tipperary, Ireland

Phone: +353 1 836 6222


## Roscrea Railway Station

Iarnród Éireann

Castleholding, Roscrea

Co. Tipperary, Ireland

Phone: +353 505 21823


## Limerick Junction Station

Iarnród Éireann

Co. Tipperary, Ireland

Phone: +353 (0) 62 51824


## Nenagh Railway Station

Iarnród Éireann

Station, Nenagh

Co. Tipperary, Ireland

Phone: +353 67 31232


## Tipperary Railway Station

Iarnród Éireann
Station Rd., Tipperary
Co. Tipperary, Ireland
Phone: +353 62 51206

## Thurles Train Station

Iarnród Éireann
The Colmyard, Thurles
Co. Tipperary, Ireland
Phone: +353 504 21733

## Templemore Railway Station

Iarnród Éireann, Templemore
Co. Tipperary, Ireland
Phone: +353 504 31342

## Westmeath County

## Athlone Railway Station

Southern Station Rd., Athlone
Co. Westmeath, Ireland
Phone: +353 (0) 90 647 3300

## Mullingar Railway Station

Green Bridge, Mullingar

Co. Westmeath, Ireland

Phone: +353 (0) 44 934 8274

## Wicklow County

## Arklow Railway Station

St. Mary's Rd., Arklow

Co. Wicklow, Ireland

Phone: +353 (0) 4 023 2519

## Bray Daly Railway Station

Florence Rd., Bra

Co. Wicklow, Ireland

Phone: +353 (0) 1 828 6305

## Greystones Railway Station

Iarnród Éireann

Church Rd., Greystones

Co. Wicklow, Ireland

Phone: +353 (0) 1 828 6340

## Kilcoole Railway Station
Iarnród Éireann, Kilcoole
Co. Wicklow, Ireland
Phone: +353 1 836 6222

## Rathdrum Railway Station
Iarnród Éireann, Rathdrum
Co. Wicklow, Ireland
Phone: +353 404 67329

## Wexford County

## Wicklow Railway Station
Iarnród Éireann
Station Rd., Wicklow
Co. Wicklow, Ireland
Phone: +353 404 67329

## Enniscorthy Railway Station
Iarnród Éireann, Enniscorthy
Co. Wexford, Ireland

Phone: +353 (0) 53 923 3488

## Gorey Railway Station

Iarnród Éireann, Gorey

Co. Wexford, Ireland

Phone: +353 (0) 53 942 1105

## RosslareEuroport Station

Iarnród Éireann, Rosslare Harbour

Co. Wexford, Ireland

Phone: +353 53 91 22522

## Waterford County

## Rosslare Strand Station

Iarnród Éireann, Rosslare Strad

Co. Wexford, Ireland

Phone: +353 53 913 2262

## Plunkett Railway Station

Iarnród Éireann

Terminus Street, Waterford

Co. Waterford, Ireland

Phone: +353 51 873401

## Train Stations in Northern Ireland

## Belfast

**Belfast Central Railway Station**
E Bridge Sreet, Belfast
County Antrim BT1 3PR, United Kingdom

**Belfast Great Victoria Street Railway Station**
Great Victoria Street
Belfast, United Kingdom

**Adelaide Railway Station**
Falcon Rd., Belfast
County Antrim BT12 6PU, United Kingdom

**Balmoral Railway Station**
484-486 Lisburn Rd.
Belfast BT9 7WD, United Kingdom

## Carnalea Railway Station

North Down BT19 1EU

Bangor, United Kingdom

## Carrickfergus Railway Station

Victoria Street, County Antrim BT38 8AQ

Carrickfergus, United Kingdom

## Castlerock Railway Station

17 Sea Rd., BT51 4TL

Coleraine, United Kingdom

# Train Stations in Italy

## Rome

### Roma Termini

Piazzela dei Cinquecento, 00185
Rome, Itlay

## Bologna

### Bolgna Centrale

Piazza delle Medaglie d'Oro, 40121
Bologna BO, Italy

## Florence

### Firenze Santa Maria Novella

Piazza della Stazione, 50123
Florence, Italy

### Firenze Campo di Marte

Via Mannelli 12
50141 Firenze FI

Florence, Itlay

**Firenze Rifredi**
Via dello Steccuto
50141 Firenze FI
Florence, Italy


**Figline Valdarno**
Piazza della Repubblica 2
Florence, Italy

**Milan**

**Milano Centrale**
Piazza Duca d'Aosta, 20124
Mialn, Italy

**Milano Porta Garibaldi**
Piazza Freud 1
Milan, Italy

**Milano Certosa**

Via Varesina 214, 20156

Milan, Italy

## Venice

## Venezia Santa Lucia

Fondamenta Santa Lucia, 30121

Venice, Italy

## Venezia Mestre

Piazzale Pietro Favretti, 30171

Venice, Italy

## Naples

## Napoli Centrale

Piazza Garibaldi, 80142

Naples, Italy

## Pisa

## Pisa Centrale

Piazza della Stazione, 56125

Pisa, Italy

## Palermo

## Palermo Centrale
Piazza Giulio Cesare, 90127
Palermo, Italy

## Padua

## Padova Railway Station
Piazza Stazione 1, 35131
Padua, Italy

## Massa

## Massa Centro
Piazza IV Novembre, 54100
Massa, Italy

## Turin

## Turin Porta Nuova

Cosro Vittorio Emanuele II, 10125
Turin, Italy

## Verona

### Verona Porta Nuova
Piazalle 25 Aprile, 6, 37138
Verona, Italy

### Arezzo

### Arezzo Railway Station
Piazza della Repubblica, 52100
Arezzo, Italy

### Livorno

### Livorno Centrale
Piazza Dante, 57124
Livorno, Italy

### Lucca

## Lucca Railway Station

Piazza Ricasole, 55100

Lucca, Italy

## Genoa

## Genova Brignole

Piazza Verdi, 16120 Genova

Genoa, Italy

## Genova Piazza Principe

Piazza Acquaverde, 16126

Genoa, Italy

## Bari

## Bari Centrale

Piazza Aldo Moro, 70122

Bari, Itlay

## Ciampino

## Ciampino Railway Station

Piazza Luigi Rizzo, 10034 Ciampino RM
Rome, Italy

## Civitavecchia

### Civitavecchia Railway Station
Viale della Repubblica, 0053 Civitavecchia RM
Rome, Italy

## Fiumicino

### Fiumicino Aerporto Railway Station
Via Generale Felice Santini 1140
00054 Fiumicino RM
Rome, Italy

## Grosseto

### Grosseto Railway Station
Piazza Guglielmo Marconi, 58100
Grosseto, Italy

# Train Stations in Luxembourg

## Belval

### Belval-Rédange Railway Station
Esch-sur-Alzette
Belval, Luxembourg

### Belval-Université Railway Station
Esch-sur-Alzette
Belval, Luxembourg

## Belvaux

### Belvaux-Soleuvre Railway Station
12 Rue de la Gare, 4460
Belvaux, Luxembourg

## Berchem

### Berchem Railway Station
18 Rue Hans Adam, 3321
Berchem, Luxembourg

## Bertrange

### Gare Bartreng-Stroossen (Bertrange-Strassen Railway Station)

Impasse Quatre Saisons, 8077
Bertrange, Luxembourg

## Bettembourg

### Gare Beetebuerg (Bettembourg Railway Station)

1014-1980 Rue de la Briquetterie, 3260
Bettembourg, Luxembourg

## Betzdorf

### Gare Betzder (Betzdorf Railway Station)

9 Rue de la Gare, 6832
Betzdorf, Luxembourg

# Train Stations in Netherlands

### Aalten (Atn)

Stationsstraat 38-40

7122 Aalten, The Netherlands

### Abcoude (Ac)

Gein Zuid 9

1391 GT Abcoude, The Netherlands

### Akkrum (Akm)

Galemaleane 24

8491 BB Akkrum, The Netherlands

### Alkmaar (Amr)

Stationsweg 45B,

1815 CB Alkmaar, The Netherlands

### Almelo (Aml)

Parallelweg 26,

7604 Almelo, The Netherlands

### Almere Centrum (Alm)

Busplein 40,

1315 KV Almere, The Netherlands

## Haarlem (Hlm)

Stationsplein 1

2011 LR Haarlem, The Netherlands

## Halfweg-Zwanenburg (Hwzb)

Teding van Berkhoutweg

1165 Halfweg, The Netherlands

## 't Harde (Hde)

Eperweg 123

8084 HD 't Harde, The Netherlands

## Hardenberg (Hdb)

Parallelweg 1-2

7772 SB Hardenberg, The Netherlands

## Harderwijk (Hd)

Stationsplein 2

3844 KR Harderwijk, The Netherlands

## Hardinxveld-Giessendam (Gnd)

Stationsstraat 21

3371 AX Hardinxveld-Giessendam, The Netherlands

## Haren (Hrn)

Stationsplein 1

9751 SX Haren, The Netherlands

## Harlingen (Hlg)

Koningin Julianastraat

8862 Harlingen, The Netherlands

## Heemskerk (Hk)

Euratomplein 1

1966 SP Heemskerk, The Netherlands

## Heemstede-Aerdenhout (Had)

Zandvoortselaan

2106 Heemstede, The Netherlands

## Heerenveen (Hr)

Stationstunnel

8441 Heerenveen, The Netherlands

**Heerhugowaard (Hwd)**

Stationsplein 3

1703 WD Heerhugowaard, The Netherlands

**Heerlen (Hrl)**

Parkeerplaats

6411 Heerlen, The Netherlands

**Heeze (Hz)**

De Leuren 19

5591 ND Heeze, The Netherlands

**Heiloo (Hlo)**

Hoog en Laag 131

1852 AX Heiloo, The Netherlands

**Heino (Hno)**

Stationsweg 31

8141 SK Heino, The Netherlands

## Helmond (Hm)

Stationsplein 3

5701 PE Helmond, The Netherlands

## Hemmen-Dodewaard (Hmn)

Boelenhamsestraat 4

6669 MN Dodewaard, The Netherlands

## Hengelo (Hgl)

Stationsplein 321

7551 CN Hengelo, The Netherlands

## 's-Hertogenbosch (Ht)

Magistratenlaan 260

5223 MA 's-Hertogenbosch, The Netherlands

## Hillegom (Hil)

2e Loosterweg 2

2182 CJ Hillegom, The Netherlands

## Hilversum (Hvs)

Stationsstraat 2B

1211 EM Hilversum, The Netherlands

**Hindeloopen (Hnp)**

Stationsweg

8713 Hindeloopen, The Netherlands

**Hoek van Holland Haven (Hld)**

Pastoor Onderwaterhof 19

3151 Hoek van Holland, The Netherlands

**Hoek van Holland Strand (Hlds)**

Strandweg 19

3151 HV Hoek van Holland, The Nether-lands

**Hoensbroek (Hb)**

Economiestraat 15

6433 KC Hoensbroek, The Netherlands

**Hoevelaken (Hvl)**

Rijksweg

3836 Stoutenburg-Noord, The Netherlands

**Hollandsche Rading (Hor)**
Vuurse Dreef 14
3739 KT Hollandsche Rading, The Netherlands

**Holten (Hon)**
Stationsstraat 10
7451 BH Holten, The Netherlands

**Hoofddorp (Hfd)**
Zuidtangent
2132 Hoofddorp, The Netherlands

**Alphen a/d Rijn (Apn)**
Stationsplein 10,
2405 BK Alphen aan den Rijn, The Netherlands

**Amersfoort (Amf)**
Stationsplein 71,

3818 LE Amersfoort, The Netherlands

## Amsterdam Centraal (Asd)

Stationsplein,

1012 AB Amsterdam, The Netherlands

## Anna Paulowna (Ana)

Kruiswijk 21,

1761 AR Anna Paulowna, The Netherlands

## Apeldoorn (Apd)

Laan van de Mensenrechten 370,

7331 VX Apeldoorn, The Netherlands

## Appingedam (Apg)

N33, 9901

Appingedam, The Netherlands

## Arkel (Akl)

Parallelweg,

4241 Arkel, The Netherlands

## Arnemuiden (Arn)

Doeleweg 7, 4341 PA

Arnemuiden, The Netherlands

## Arnhem (Ah)

Nieuwe Stationsstraat 10,

6811 Arnhem, The Netherlands

## Assen (Asn)

Stationsplein 3,

9401 LB Assen,The Netherlands

## Gaanderen (Gdr)

Hoofdstraat 27

7011 AA Gaanderen, The Netherlands

## Geerdijk (Gdk)

Geerdijk 65

7681 SC Vroomshoop, The Netherlands

## Geldermalsen (Gdm)

Trichtsevoetpad 1

4191 LA Geldermalsen, The Netherlands

## Geldrop (Gp)

Parallelweg 18

5664 AD Geldrop, The Netherlands

## Geleen Oost (Gln)

Stationstraat 15-16

6166 CB Geleen, The Netherlands

## Gilze-Rijen (Gz)

Parallelweg 20

5121 Rijen, The Netherlands

## Glanerbrug (Gbr)

Vijverstraat

7532 Enschede, The Netherlands

## Goes (Gs)

Stationspark

4462 Goes, The Netherlands

## Goor (Go)

Stationslaan 14-16

7471 AP Goor, The Netherlands

## Gorinchem (Gr)

Stationsplein 42

3364 AM Sliedrecht, The Netherlands

## Gouda (Gd)

Burgemeester Jamesplein 2

2803 PG Gouda, The Netherlands

## Gramsbergen (Gbg)

De Oostermaat 48

7783 BX Gramsbergen, The Netherlands

## Grijpskerk (Gk)

Stationsstraat 29-30

9843 AE Grijpskerk, The Netherlands

## Groningen (Gn)

Stationsplein 26

9726 AE Groningen, The Netherlands

## Grou-Jirnsum (Gw)

Reinerswei 3

9001 ZL Grou, The Netherlands

## Baarn (Brn)

Prinses Marielaan 2

3743 JA Baarn, The Netherlands

## Baflo (Bf)

Sasmaweg 1

9953 RV Baflo, The Netherlands

## Barendrecht (Brd)

Zuideinde

2991 Barendrecht, The Netherlands

## Barneveld Centrum (Bnc)

Stationsplein 4

3771 ES Barneveld, The Netherlands

## Bedum (Bdm)

Parallelweg

9781 Bedum, The Netherlands

## Beek-Elsloo (Bk)

Sanderboutlaan 3

6181 DN Elsloo, The Netherlands

## Beesd (Bsd)

Stationsweg 2

4153 RD Beesd, The Netherlands

## Beilen (Bl)

Stationslaan 11

9411 PS Beilen, The Netherlands

## Bergen op Zoom (Bgn)

Spoortunneltje

4621 Bergen op Zoom, The Netherlands

## Best (Bet)

Spoorstraat 3

5684 AA Best, The Netherlands

## Beverwijk (Bv)

Stationsplein 46B

1948 LC Beverwijk, The Netherlands

**Bilthoven (Bhv)**

Julianalaan 1-3

3722 GA Bilthoven, The Netherlands

**Blerick (Br)**

Kazernestraat 3

5928 NL Venlo, The Netherlands

**Bloemendaal (Bll)**

Zuider Stationsweg 20

2061 HE Bloemendaal, The Netherlands

**Bodegraven (Bdg)**

Stationsplein 3

2411 EH Bodegraven, The Netherlands

**Borne (Bn)**

Ruwerstraat 116

7621 SV Borne, The Netherlands

**Boskoop (Bsk)**

Parklaan 8-10

2771 GB Boskoop, The Netherlands

## Bovenkarspel Flora (Bkf)

Burgemeester van Bredastraat 1

1611 CR Bovenkarspel, The Netherlands

## Bovenkarspel-Grootebroek (Bkg)

De Kuil 2

1611 KS Bovenkarspel, The Netherlands

## Boxmeer (Bmr)

Stationsweg 1

5831 CR Boxmeer, The Netherlands

## Boxtel (Btl)

Traverse

5281 Boxtel, The Netherlands

## Breda (Bd)

Stationsplein 16

4811 BB Breda, The Netherlands

## Breukelen (Bkl)

Stationsweg 105

3621 LK Breukelen, The Netherlands

## Brummen (Bmn)

Stationsweg 1

6971 BX Brummen, The Netherlands

## Buitenpost (Bp)

Stationsplein 2

9285 VW Buitenpost, The Netherlands

## Bunde (Bde)

Spoorstraat 8

6241 CL Bunde, The Netherlands

## Bunnik (Bnk)

Groeneweg 128

3981 CN Bunnik, The Netherlands

## Bussum Zuid (Bsmz)

Struikheiweg 5

1406 TK Bussum, The Netherlands

**Echt (Ec)**

Stationsweg 5A

6101 HK Echt, The Netherlands

**Ede-Wageningen (Ed)**

Stationsplein 8

6711 PN Ede, The Netherlands

**Eindhoven (Ehv)**

Eindhoven Station

Eindhoven, The Netherlands

**Elst (Est)**

Aamsestraat 20

6662 Elst, The Netherlands

**Emmen (Emn)**

Stationsplein 10A

7811 GC Emmen, The Netherlands

**Enkhuizen (Ekz)**

Bosmankade

1601 Enkhuizen, The Netherlands

**Enschede (Es)**

Stationsplein 33I

7511 JD Enschede, The Netherlands

**Ermelo (Eml)**

Dokter van Dalelaan 7

3851 JA Ermelo, The Netherlands

**Etten-Leur (Etn)**

Stationsplein 3

4872 XL Etten-Leur, The Netherlands

**Franeker (Fn)**

Parallelweg 7-9

8801 JM Franeker, The Netherlands

**Capelle Schollevaar (Cps)**

Picassopassage 17

2907 ME, The Netherlands

## Castricum (Cas)

Beverwijkerstraatweg 32a

1901 NJ Castricum, The Netherlands

## Coevorden (Co)

Parallelweg 20

7741 KB Coevorden, The Netherlands

## Cuijk (Ck)

Stationsplein 3

5431 CE Cuijk, The Netherlands

## Culemborg (Cl)

Stationsplein 1

4101 NX Culemborg, The Netherlands

## Daarlerveen (Da)

Grote Veenweg 2-4

7687 AV Daarlerveen, The Netherlands

**Dalen (Dln)**

Kymmelskampen 3

7751 GN Dalen, The Netherlands

**Dalfsen (Dl)**

Heinoseweg 1

7722 JM Dalfsen, The Netherlands

**Deinum (Dei)**

Spoorstrjitte 18

9033 WJ Deinum, The Netherlands

**Delden (Ddn)**

Stationsweg 5

7491 CE Delden, The Netherlands

**Delft (Dt)**

Van Leeuwenhoeksingel 59

2611 AD Delft, The Netherlands

**Delfzijl (Dz)**

Damsterlaan

9934 Delfzijl, The Netherlands

**Den Dolder (Dld)**
Dolderseweg 99
3734 BE Den Dolder, The Netherlands

**Den Haag Centraal (Gvc) (The Hague)**
Prins Clauslaan 24
2595 AJ Den Haag, The Netherlands

**Den Helder (Hdr)**
Middenweg 176
1782 BL Den Helder, The Netherlands

**Deurne (Dn)**
Fabriekstraat 16
5753 AH Deurne, The Netherlands

**Deventer (Dv)**
Stationsplein 6
7411 HB Deventer, The Netherlands

## Didam (Did)

Stationsplein

6942 Didam, The Netherlands

## Diemen (Dmn)

Dokter A.J.j. van Gemertplein 1

1111 LZ Diemen, The Netherlands

## Dieren (Dr)

Stationsplein 5

6953 AA Dieren, The Netherlands

## Doetinchem (Dtc)

Stationsplein 8

7005 AK Doetinchem, The Netherlands

## Dordrecht (Ddr)

Stationsplein 1

3311 JV Dordrecht, The Netherlands

## Driebergen-Zeist (Db)

Stationsplein

3972 Driebergen-Rijsenburg, The Netherlands

## Driehuis (Dh)
Van den Vondellaan 100
1985 BD Driehuis, The Netherlands

## Dronrijp (Drp)
Hatzum 2
9035 VK Dronryp, The Netherlands

## Dronten (Dron)
Het Kamp 4
8251 GK Dronten, The Netherlands

## Duiven (Dvn)
Parallelweg 32
6922 HR Duiven, The Netherlands

## Duivendrecht (Dvd)
Pablo Nerudalaan
1115 Duivendrecht, The Netherlands

# Train Stations in Norway

## Oslo

### Oslo Central Station
Jernbanetorget 1, 0154
Oslo, Norway

## Arendal

### Rise stasjon
Rise, 4848
Arendal, Norway

### Bråstad stasjon
4848 Bråstad
Arendal, Norway

## Blakstad

### Blakstad stasjon
4820 Froland
Blakstad, Norway

# Train Stations in Poland

## Warszawa Centralna
Al. Jerozolimskie 54, Śródmieście,
Warsaw, Masovian, Poland

## Warszawa Gdańska
Zygmunta Słomińskiego 4, 00-204
Warsaw, Poland

## Warszawa Ochota
Ochota, Warsaw
Masovian, Poland

## Warszawa Powiśle
Aleja 3 Maja, Powiśle, Warsaw
Masovian, Poland

## Kraków Główny Osobowy
Lesser Poland Voivodeship
Kraków, Poland

## Białystok Railway Station

Podlaskie Voivodeship
Białystok, Poland

**Bydgoszcz Główna**
Kuyavian-Pomeranian Voivodeship
Bydgoszcz, Poland

**Katowice Railway Station**
City center, Silesian Voivodeship
Katowice, Poland

**Lublin Główny**
Za Cukrownią, Lublin Voivodeship
Lublin, Poland

**Łódź Fabryczna**
City center, Łódź Voivodeship
Łódź, Poland

**Łódź Kaliska**
Łódź, Poland

# Opole

## Opole Główne

City center, Opole Voivodeship

Opole, Poland

## Poznań Główny

Dworcowa Street 1, Greater Poland Voivodeship

Poznań, Poland

## Szczecin

Szczecin Główny

West Pomeranian

Szczecin, Poland

## Sopt Railway Station

Sopt, Poland

## Gdynia

Gdynia Główna

City center, Pomeranian Voivodeship

Gdynia, Poland

## Gdańsk Główny

Podwale Grodzkie Street, City centre, Pomeranian Voivodeship

Gdańsk, Poland

## Gdańsk Oliwa

Oliwa

Gdańsk, Poland

## Wrocław Główny

Pilsudskiego Street, Lower Silesian Voivodeship

Wrocław, Poland

# Train Stations in Portugal

## Lisbon

Estação de Caminhos de Ferro do Rossio
(Rossio Railway Station)
Main façade towards Rossio Square
Lisbon, Portugal

## Estação comboio Campolide

Calçada Estação, 1070-025
Lisbon, Portugal
Phone: +351 808 208 208

# Train Stations in Romania

## Braşov Railway Station
B-dul Gării, Nr. 1
Braşov, Romania

## Bucureşti Gara de Nord (Bucharest North Railway Station)
Piaţa Gării de Nord, Bucharest, Romania
Gara Barsab (Basarb Railway Station)
Bucharest, Romania

## Cluj-Napoca
Gara Centrală (Central Railway Station)
Piaţa Gării 2-3, 400000
Cluj-Napoca, Romania

## Constanţa Railway Station
Strada Gării
Constanţa, Romania

## Iaşi Railway Station
Piaţa Gării

Iași, Romania

**Sibiu Central Railway Station**
Piața 1 Decembrie 1918 6
Sibiu, Romania

**Sinaia Railway Station**
Calea Prahovei
Sinaia, Romania

**Timișoara Nord Railway Station**
Strada Gării, Nr. 2
Timișoara, Romania

**Gara Craiova**
Craiova, Romania

**Satu Mare Railway Station**
Satu Mare, Romania

# Train Stations in Russia

## Moscow

### Leningradsky Railway Station
3 Komsomolskaya Square,
Moscow, Russia
Phone: (+7) 495 262 91 43

### Yaroslavsky Railway Station
5 Komsomolskaya Square,
Moscow, Russia
Phone: (+7) 800 775 00 00

### Kazansky Railway Station
Komsomolskaya Square,
Moscow, Russia
Phone: (+7) 499 266 31 81

### Belorussky Railway Station
Tverskaya Zastava Square,
Moscow,Russia
Phone:  (+7) 495 251 60 93

**Kursky Railway Station**

Kursky Station Square,

Moscow, Russia

(+7) 495 266 53 10

**Savyolovsky Railway Station**

Savyolovsky Station Square,

Moscow,Russia

Phone: (+7) 499 266 89 01

**Paveletsky Railway Station**

Paveletskaya Square,

Moscow, Russia

Phone: (+7) 495 235 05 22

**Rizhsky Railway Station**

Rizhskaya Square,

Moscow, Russia

Phone: (+7) 495 631 15 88

**Kiyevsky Railway Station**

Kiyevsky Station Square,

Moscow, Russia

Phone:   (+7) 499 240 04 15

Saint Petersburg

## Moskovsky Railway Station

85, Nevsky av., St. Petersburg, Russia

Phone:   (+7) 812 457 44 28

## Vitebsky Railway Station

32, Zagorodny av.

St. Petersburg, Russia

Phone:   (+7) 812 457 59 39

## Baltiysky Railway Station

120, Nab. Obvodnogo Kanala,

St. Petersburg, Russia

Phone:   (+7) 812 457 28 59

## Finland Station

5 Lenin Square,

Saint Petersburg, Russia

Phone:   (+7) 812 436 67 46

## Ladozhsky Railway Station

73, Zanevsky Prospekt,

St. Petersburg,Russia

Phone:   (+7) 812 436 53 10

# Train Stations in Spain

## A Coruña

### San Diego A Coruña Railway Station
Avenida do Ejército, 15006
A Coruña, Spain

### San Cristóbal A Coruña Railway Station
Ronda de Outeiro, 15007
A Coruña, Spain

### Albacete Railway Station
Avda de la Estación, 02001
Albacete, Spain

### A Gudiña Railway Station
Rúa Beato Sebastián de Aparicio 163, 32540
A Gudiña, Ourense, Spain

### Almansa Railway Station
Plaza Primero de Mayo, 02640

Almansa, Spain

**Alicante Terminal Railway Station**
Avenida de la Estación,
03005
Alicante, Spain

**Elx-Parc Railway Station**
Av Ferrocarril 4,
03202
Elche, Alicante, Spain

**Elx-Carrús Railway Station**
Carrer Oscar Esplá 92-94,
03201
Elx, Alacant, Spain

**Algercias Railway Station**
Calle de José Fariña,
11207
Algeciras, Spain

**Port of Algeciras**

Acera de la Marina, 11201

Algeciras, Spain

**Alcázar de San Juan Railway Station**

Av Álvarez Guerra 28, 13600

Alcázar de San Juan,

Ciudad Real, Spain

**Albacete Railway Station**

Avda de la Estación, 02001

Albacete, Spain

**Almería Railway Station**

Plaza de la Estación,

04006

Almería, Spain

**Port of Almería**

Calle de Nicolás Salmerón,

04002

Almería, Spain

**Antequera**

## Antequera Railway Station

Barriada Estación,

29200

Antequera, Málaga, Spain

## Arcos de Jalón

## Arcos de Jalón Railway Station

Calle Ferrocarril,

42250

Arcos de Jalón, Soria, Spain

## Ávila Railway Station

Paseo de la Estación 42,

05001

Ávila, Spain

## Badajoz Railway Station

Argüello Carvajal Teologo Siglo

XVII, 10, 06007

Badajoz, Spain

# Barcelona

## Port of Barcelona

Moll 18 C,

08039

Barcelona, Spain

## Glòries

Ildefons Cerdà

La Bonanova

Via Augusta,

Barcelona

Tel: +34 932 54 09 54

## El Clot-Aragó

Plaça de Font i Sagué, 3,

08018

Barcelona, Spain

Tel: +34 932 45 29 47

## Barcelona Sants Railway Station

Plaça de Sants,

08014

Barcelona, Spain

## Barcelona Sagrera Railway Station
Carrer del Pont del Treball,
08020
Barcelona, Spain

## Barcelona França Railway Station
Avinguda del Marquès de l'Argentera, 6,
08003
Barcelona, Spain

## L-Hospitalet de Llobregat Railway Station
Rambla Just Oliveras,
08901
L'Hospitalet de Llobregat, Barcelona, Spain

## Badalona Railway Station
Plaça Roca i Pi 1,
08912
Badalona, Barcelona, Spain

## Sabadell Centre Railway Station

08202 Sabadell,

Barcelona, Spain

**Mataró Railway Station**

Avinguda del Maresme,

08301 Mataró,

Barcelona, Spain

**Santa Coloma de Gramenet Metro Station**

Plaça Vila, 08921

Santa Coloma de Gramenet,

Barcelona, Spain

**Terrassa Railway Station**

Plaça Estació del Nord,

08221 Terrassa,

Barcelona, Spain

**Benicarló - Peníscola Railway Station**

Passeig de l'Estacio,

12580

Benicarló, Spain

**Benicàssim Railway Station**

Avenida Mediterráneo,

12560

Benicasim, Spain

**Bilbao Abando - RENFE Railway Station**

Calle Hurtado de Amezaga 8,

48008

Bilbao, Spain

**Bilbao Atxuri Euskotren Railway Station**

Atxuri Kalea, 48006

Bilbao, Spain

**Bilbao Concordia - FEVE Railway Station**

Estación de La Concordia de Bilbao (FEVE),

48001

Bilbao, Spain

**Blanes Railway Station**

Avinguda Estació,

17300

Blanes, Girona, Spain

## Bobadilla Railway Station

Calle Estación Renfe,

29540

Bobadilla, Antequera, Spain

## Burgos

## Railway Station Burgos Rosa de Lima

Avenida Principes de Asturias,

09006

Burgos, Spain

## Miranda de Ebro Railway Station

Plaza de la Estación,

09200

Miranda de Ebro, Burgos, Spain

## Cáceres Railway Station

Avenida de la Hispanidad,

10005

Cáceres, Spain

**Cadiz Railway Station**
Plaza de Sevilla 1,
11006
Cádiz, Spain

**Port of Cadiz**
Av del Puerto,
11006
Cádiz, Spain

**Calella Railway Station**
Carrer Anselm Clavé 158-168,
08370
Calella, Spain

**Cartagena Railway Station**
Calle de Tirso de Molina,
30203
Cartagena, Spain

**Castellón de la Plana Railway Station**

Plaza Victor Falomir,

12006

Castellón de la Plana, Castelló, Spain

**Castellón de la Plana Railway Station**

Plaza Victor Falomir,

12006

Castellón de la Plana, Castelló, Spain

**Ceuta**

**Port of Ceuta**

51001

Ceuta, Spain

**Ciudad Real Central Railway Station**

Calle Santa María de Alarcos,

13005

Ciudad Real, Spain

**Ciudad Rodrigo Railway Station**

Paseo Estación 55,

37500

Ciudad Rodrigo, Salamanca, Spain

**Córdoba Central Railway Station**
Glorieta de las Tres Culturas,
S/N 14011
Córdoba, Spain

**Almonaster la Real**

**Almonaster-Cortegana Railway Station**
21342
Almonaster la Real, Spain

**Cuenca Railway Station**
Calle Mariano Catalina,
16004
Cuenca, Spain

**San Sebastián-Donostia Railway Station**
Paseo de Francia,
2220012
San Sebastián, Spain

## Dos Hermanas Railway Station

Plaza Arenal 1,

41701

Dos Hermanas, Sevilla, Spain

## Figueres Vilafant Railway Station

Carrer de Marià Fortuny, 24,

17600

Figueres, Spain

## Figueres Railway Station

Plaça de l'Estació,

17600

Figueres, Spain

## Madrid

## Fuenlabrada Railway Station

Paseo Estación,

28944

Fuenlabrada, Madrid, Spain

## Getafe Central Railway Station

Calle Dee La Estación,
28904
Getafe, Madrid, Spain

## Royal Palace of Madrid
Calle Bailén,
 28071
Madrid, Spain

## Madrid Chamartín Railway Station
Estación de Chamartín,
 28046
Madrid, Spain
Tel: +34 902 24 02 02.

## Leganés Railway Station
Calle Virgen del Camino,
28911
Leganés, Madrid, Spain

## Madrid Puerta de Atocha Railway Station
28014

Glorieta Carlos

Madrid, Spain

Phone: +34 902 243 402

**Móstoles Railway Station**

Paseo de la Estación,

28933

Móstoles, Madrid, Spain

**Torrejón de Ardoz Railway Station**

Paseo Estación, 28850

Torrejón de Ardoz, Madrid, Spain

**Alcalá de Henares Railway Station**

Plaza de la Estación,

28807

Alcalá de Henares, Madrid, Spain

**Alcorcón Central Railway Station**

Avenida de Móstoles,

28922

Alcorcón, Madrid, Spain

## Alcalá de Henares Railway Station

Plaza de la Estación,

28807

Alcalá de Henares, Madrid, Spain

## Gijón Railway Station

Calle Carlos Marx,

33207

Gijón, Asturias, Spain

## Girona Railway Station

Plaça d'Espanya, 4,

17002

Girona, Spain

## Granada Railway Station

Calle Doctor Jaime Garcia Royo,

18014

Granada, Spain

## Granollers Central Railway Station

Carrer Llevant,

08402

Granollers, Spain

## Guadalajara-Yebes Railway Station
19139
Guadalajara, Spain

## Sigüenza Railway Station
Carretera de Soria,
19250
Sigüenza, Guadalajara, Spain

## Guadalajara Railway Station
Plaza Estación,
19004 Guadalajara, Spain

## Guadix Railway Station
Av Estación 8-12,
18500
Guadix, Spain

## Guillarei Railway Station
36720
Guillarei, Pontevedra, Spain

## Huesca Railway Station

Calle José Gil Cávez,

22005 Huesca, Spain

## Irun EUSKOTREN Railway Station

Paseo Colón 52,

20301

Irun, Guipúzcoa, Spain

## Irun RENFE Railway Station

Geltoki Kalea,

20301

Irun, Spain

## Jaén

## Baeza Railway Station

Plaza de las Palmeras,

23490

Estación Linares-Baeza, Jaén, Spain

## Jaén Railway Station

Plaza de la Concordia,

23008

Jaén, Spain

**Linares-Baeza Railway Station**

Plaza de las Palmeras,

23490

Estación Linares-Baeza, Jaén, Spain

**Jerez de la Frontera Railway Station**

Plaza de la Estación,

11401

Jerez de la Frontera, Cádiz, Spain

**Huelva**

**Huelva Término Railway Station**

Avenida de Italia,

21003

Huelva, Spain

**La Puebla de Híjar Railway Station**

Plaza Reino de Aragón 1,

44510

La Estación - La Puebla de Híjar, Teruel, Spain

**Málaga-María Zambrano Railway Station**

Calle Explanada de la Estación, 29002

Málaga, Spain

**Marbella Bus Station**

Avenida del Trapiche, 29602

Marbella, Málaga, Spain

**León Railway Station**

Calle Astorga, 24009

León, Spain

**Sevilla**

**Marchena Railway Station**

Av Maestro Santos Ruano,

41620 Marchena, Sevilla, Spain

## Sevilla Avda.

de Kansas City

Seville Andalusia Spain

+34 902 210 317

## Lleida Pirineus Railway Station

Plaça de L'Edil Saturni,

25007

Lleida, Spain

## Lloret de Mar Bus Station

Avinguda Vila de Blanes,

17310

Lloret de Mar, Spain

## Logroño Railway Station

Av de Lobete,

26006

Logroño, La Rioja, Spain

## Loja San Francisco Railway Station

Calle de Renfe,

18300

Loja, Spain

## Lugo Railway Station

Plaza Conde de Fontao,

27297

Lugo, Spain

## Monforte de Lemos Railway Station

Plaza Estación,

27400

Monforte de Lemos, Lugo, Spain

## La Molina Railway Station

17537 Alp, Spain

## Medina del Campo Railway Station

Av Estación 23,

47400

Medina del Campo, Spain

## Murcia del Carmen Railway Station

Plaza Industria 1,

30002

Murcia, Spain

## Maçanet de la Selva
## Maçanet-Massanes Railway Station

Estación Maçanet-Massanes,

17412

Maçanet de la Selva, Spain

## O Porriño Railway Station

Rúa Estación,

36400

O Porriño, Pontevedra, Spain

## Ourense Railway Station

Rúa Eulogio Gómez Franqueira,

32001

Ourense, Spain

## Oviedo Railway Station

Plaza de los Ferroviarios,

33012

Oviedo, Asturias, Spain

**Palencia Railway Station**

Calle Estación Norte,

34005

Palencia, Spain

**Palma de Mallorca**

**Port of Palma de Mallorca**

Avinguda Gabriel Roca,

07015

Palma de Mallorca, Illes Balears, Spain

**Pamplona**

**Pamplona Railway Station**

Calle de la Estación,

31012

Pamplona, Navarra, Spain

**Pontevedra Railway Station**

Rúa Eduardo Pondal,
36003
Pontevedra, Spain

**Redondela de Galicia Railway Station**
36800
Redondela, Pontevedra, Spain

**Portbou Railway Station**
Carrer de Claudi Planás 3,
17497
Portbou, Spain

**Puerto de la Cruz**

**Bus Station Puerto de la Cruz**
Calle Pozo, 0 S/N,
38400
Puerto de la Cruz, Spain

**Puertollano**

## Puertollano Railway Station

Calle Muelle,

13500

Puertollano, Ciudad Real, Spain

## Puigcerdà Railway Station

Carrer de L´Éstacio,

17520

Puigcerdà, Spain

## Ribadavia Railway Station

Rúa Baixada o Consello,

32400

Ribadavia, Ourense, Spain

## Ribes de Freser Railway Station

17534

Ribes de Freser, Spain

## Ripoll Railway Station

Carrer Progrés,

17500

Ripoll, Spain

# Ronda

### Ronda Railway Station

Av Andalucía,

29400

Ronda, Málaga, Spain

### Sagunt Railway Station

Avinguda del País Valencià,

46500 Sagunt, Spain

### Salamanca Railway Station

Plaza de la Estación,

37004

Salamanca, Spain

### Fuentes de Oñoro Railway Station

Calle Gabriel y Galán,

37481

Fuentes de Oñoro, Salamanca, Spain

### San Roque - La Linea Railway Station

Carretera Guadarranque,

11368

San Roque, Spain

**Soria Railway Station**

42005

Soria, Spain

**Seville Santa Justa Railway Station**

Avenida de José Laguillo, Spain

**Segovia Railway Station**

Carretera Villacastín 6,

40006 Segovia, Spain

**Segovia Railway Station**

Carretera Villacastín 6,

40006

Segovia, Spain

**Santiago de Compostela Railway Station**

Av de Lugo,

15701

Santiago de Compostela, Spain

## Santander Railway Station
Calle Atilano Rodríguez,
39002
Santander, Cantabria, Spain

## Santa Cruz

## Port of Santa Cruz de Tenerife
38002
Santa Cruz de Tenerife, Spain

## Tortosa Railway Station
Carrer de Miguel de Cervantes,
43500
Tortosa, Spain

## Tarragona

## Torredembarra Railway Station
Passeig de Miramar,
43830

Torredembarra, Tarragona, Spain

## Reus Railway Station

Plaça Estació,

43202

Reus, Tarragona, Spain

## Flix Railway Station

Carrwe del Molí,

43750

Flix, Tarragona, Spain

## San Vicente de Calders Railway Station

Carrer Estació,

43880

El Vendrell, Tarragona, Spain

## Tarragona Railway Station

Plaça de la Pedrera,

43004

Tarragona, Spain

**Salou Railway Station**

Carrer de Carles Roig,

43840

Salou, Tarragona, Spain

**Toledo Railway Station**

Paseo Rosa,

45006

Toledo, Spain

**Talavera de la Reina Railway Station**

Paseo de la Estación,

45600

Talavera de la Reina, Toledo, Spain

**Vitoria-Gasteiz Railway Station**

La Estación Plazatxoa 1,

01005

Vitoria, Araba, Spain

**Teruel Railway Station**

Camino Estación,

44001

Teruel, Spain

## Xàtiva Railway Station
Av Ausiàs March,
46800
Xàtiva, Spain

## Zamora Railway Station
Carretera Estación 25,
49010
Zamora, Spain

## Vilanova i la Geltrú Railway Station
Plaça Edua Maristany,
08800
Vilanova i la Geltrú, Spain

## Valladolid-Campo Grande Railway Station
Calle Estación del Norte,
47007
Valladolid, Spain

## Vic Railway Station

Plaça Estació,

08500

Vic, Spain

## Vigo-Guixar Railway Station

Plaza Estación 1,

36201

Vigo, Pontevedra, Spain

## Valencia de Alcántara Railway Station

Poblado Estación Ferrocarril,

10500

Valencia de Alcántara, Cáceres, Spain

## Buñol Railway Station

Carretera de la Estación,

46360

Buñol, Valencia, Spain

## Valencia Joaquín Sorolla Railway Station

Calle San Vicente Mártir,

46007 Valencia, Spain

**Valencia Norte Railway Station**
46007
Valencia, Spain

**Zamora**

**Puebla de Sanabria Railway Station**
Carretera Estación,
49300
Puebla de Sanabria, Zamora, Spain

**Zaragoza**

**Zaragoza Delicias Railway Station**
50011
Zaragoza, Spain

**Calatayud Railway Station**
Explanada Estación,
50300
Calatayud, Zaragoza, Spain

**Caspe Railway Station**

Plaza Obispo Cubeles,
50700
Caspe, Zaragoza, Spain

**Quinto Railway Station**

Camino de la Estación,
50770
Quinto, Zaragoza, Spain

# Train Stations in Sweden

## Jämtland County

### Åre Railway Station

Sankt Olavs väg, 830 13

Åre, Åre Municipality

Sweden

## Kiruna

### Kiruna Central Railway Station

Bangårdsvägen, 981 34 Kiruna, Sweden

Kiruna, Sweden

Abisko

### Abisko Östra Railway Station,

981 07 Abisko, Sweden

Abisko Turiststation Railway Station,

981 07 Abisko, Sweden

## Alingsås

**Alingsås Railway Station,**

Stationsgatan 7, 441 30

Alingsås, Sweden

**Alvesta**

**Alvesta Railway Station**

Centralplan, 342 30

Alvesta, Sweden

**Ängelholm**

**Ängelholm Railway Station**

Industrigatan,

262 63

Ängelholm, Sweden

**Ånge**

**Ånge Railway Station**

Järnvägsgatan,

841 33

Ånge, Sweden

# Åmål

## Railway Station Åmål

Bondegatan 2, 662 30
Åmål, Sweden

# Älvsbyn

## Älvsbyn Railway Station

Stationsgatan,
942 33
Älvsbyn, Sweden

# Älvho

## Älvho Railway Station

Älvovägen,
794 98
Orsa, Sweden

# Arvidsjaur

## Arvidsjaur Railway Station

Järnvägsgatan

70, 933 32

Arvidsjaur, Sweden

## Arvika

## Arvika Railway Station

Järnvägsgatan

27, 671 31

Arvika, Sweden

## Åsarna

## Åsarna Railway Station

Olstavägen,

840 31

Åsarna, Sweden

## Bålsta

## Bålsta Railway Station

Stationsvägen

2, 746 32
Bålsta, Sweden

**Bastuträsk**

**Bastuträsk Railway Station**
Östra Järnvägsgatan
12, 930 61
Bastuträsk, Sweden

**Björkliden**

**Björkliden Railway Station**
Björklidenvägen
40, 981 93
Björkliden, Sweden

**Björnidet**

**Björnidet Railway Station**
794 98
Orsa, Sweden

## Boden

### Boden Central Railway Station
Stationsgatan,
 961 61
Boden, Sweden

## Borås

### Borås Central Railway Station
Stationsgatan
16, 503 38
Borås, Sweden

## Borlänge

### Borlänge Central Railway Station
Ovanbrogatan 7,
784 33
Borlänge, Sweden

## Bräcke

**Bräcke Railway Station**
Riksvägen 34,
840 60
Bräcke, Sweden

**Charlottenberg**

**Charlottenberg Railway Station**
Stationsgatan,
673 32 Charlottenberg, Sweden

**Degerfors**

**Degerfors Railway Station**
Stationsvägen 1,
693 32
Degerfors, Sweden

**Dorotea**

**Dorotea Railway Station**
Järnvägsgatan,
917 31

Dorotea, Sweden

## Duved

## Duved Railway Station

Stinsvägen 12,

830 15

Duved, Sweden

## Eskilstuna

## Eskilstuna Central Railway Station

Järnvägsplan 1,

 632 20

Eskilstuna, Sweden

## Fågelsjö

## Fågelsjö Railway Station

820 50

Los, Sweden

## Falkenberg

## Falkenberg Railway Station

Stationsgatan 18,

311 34

Falkenberg, Sweden

## Falköping

## Falköping Central Railway Station

Järnvägsgatan,

521 33

Falköping, Sweden

## Falun

## Falun Central Railway Station

Promenaden 1,

791 30

Falun, Sweden

## Gällivare

## Gällivare Railway Station

Centralplan,

982 36

Gällivare, Sweden

## Gävle

### Gävle Central Railway Station

Centralplan,

803 11

Gävle, Sweden

## Gothenburg

### Gothenburg Central Railway Station

Nils Ericsonsplatsen,

411 03

Göteborg, Sweden

## Grums

### Grums Railway Station

Sveagatan 100,

664 34

Grums, Sweden

## Hallsberg

### Hallsberg Railway Station
Stationsplan 1,
694 31
Hallsberg, Sweden

## Halmstad

### Halmstad Central Railway Station
Stationsgatan 25,
302 45
Halmstad, Sweden

## Haparanda

### Haparanda Railway Station
Järnvägsgatan 21B,
953 37
Haparanda, Sweden

## Haparanda Bus Station

Norra Esplanaden 4,

953 31

Haparanda, Sweden


## Härnösand

### Härnösand Railway Station

Järnvägsgatan 7,

871 45

Härnösand, Sweden


## Hässleholm

### Hässleholm Central Railway Station

Järnvägsgatan,

281 31

Hässleholm, Sweden


## Helsingborg

### Port of Helsingborg, Terminalgatan

252 78

Helsingborg, Sweden

## Helsingborg Central Railway Station

Järnvägsgatan 10,

252 78

Helsingborg, Sweden

## Herrljunga

## Herrljunga Railway Station

Järnvägsplatsen 1,

524 30

Herrljunga, Sweden

## Högsby

## Högsby Railway Station

Järnvägsgatan,

579 30

Högsby, Sweden

## Hoting

**Hoting Railway Station**

Järnvägsgatan 24,

830 80 Hoting, Sweden

**Jokkmokk**

**Jokkmokk Railway Station**

Stationsgatan 8A,

962 31

Jokkmokk, Sweden

**Jönköping**

**Jönköping Central Railway Station**

Järnvägsgatan 12,

553 15

Jönköping, Sweden

**Kalmar**

**Kalmar Central Railway Station**

Stationsgatan 5,

392 32

Kalmar, Sweden

## Karlskrona

### Karlskrona Central Railway Station

Blekingegatan 1 ,

371 34

Karlskrona, Sweden

## Karlstad

### Karlstad Central Railway Station

Hamngatan 21,

652 25

Karlstad, Sweden

## Katrineholm

### Katrineholm Central Railway Station

Stationsplan,

641 45

Katrineholm, Sweden

**Kil**

**Kil Railway Station**
Stationsplan 3,
665 30
Kil, Sweden

**Kiruna**

**Kiruna Central Railway Station**
Bangårdsvägen,
981 34
Kiruna, Sweden

**Kitajaur**

**Kitajaur Railway Station**
962 05
Kåbdalis, Sweden

**Kristinehamn**

## Kristinehamn Railway Station

Stationsgatan 2,

681 30

Kristinehamn, Sweden

## Kungsbacka

## Kungsbacka Railway Station

Storgatan 20A,

434 32

Kungsbacka, Sweden

## Lund

## Lund Central Railway Station

Bangatan 1,

222 21

Lund, Sweden

## Luleå

## Luleå Bus Station

Skeppsbrogatan 54,

972 31 Luleå,

Sweden, Sweden

## Luleå Central Railway Station

Prästgatan 20,

972 34

Luleå, Sweden

## Ljungskile

## Ljungskile Railway Station

Vällebergsvägen 14,

459 30

Ljungskile, Sweden

## Lit

## Lit Railway Station

Nybyvägen,

830 30 Lit, Sweden

## Linköping

## Linköping Central Railway Station

Järnvägsgatan 3,

582 22

Linköping, Sweden

## Långsele

## Långsele Railway Station

Stationsgatan 4,

882 30

Långsele, Sweden

## Landskrona

## Landskrona Railway Station

Östervångsplan 10-12,

261 44

Landskrona, Sweden

## Laholm

## Laholm Railway Station

Industrigatan 48,

312 34

Laholm, Sweden

## Malmö

## Malmö Central Railway Station

Centralplan,

211 20

Malmö, Sweden

## Mellerud

## Mellerud Railway Station

Järnvägsgatan 7,

464 30

Mellerud, Sweden

## Meselefors

## Meselefors Railway Station

Meselefors 48,

912 90

Vilhelmina, Sweden

# Mjölby

## Mjölby Railway Station
Järnvägsgatan 11,
595 52
Mjölby, Sweden

# Mölndal

## Mölndal Railway Station
Nämndemansgatan 1,
431 33
Mölndal, Sweden

# Mora

## Mora Railway Station
Stationsvägen 3,
792 32
Mora, Sweden

# Moskosel

## Moskosel Railway Station

Abmorvägen,

930 86

Moskosel, Sweden

## Murjek

## Murjek Railway Station

Järnvägsvägen,

960 33

Murjek, Sweden

## Nässjö

## Nässjö Central Railway Station

Järnvägsgatan 9,

571 31

Nässjö, Sweden

## Norrköping

## Norrköping Central Railway Station

Norra Promenaden,

602 22

Norrköping, Sweden

## Nyköping

### Nyköping Central Railway Station

Södra Bangårdsgatan,

611 30

Nyköping, Sweden

## Örebro

### Örebro Central Railway Station

Östra Bangatan 1,

703 61

Örebro, Sweden

## Orns

### Örnsköldsvik Railway Station

Bangatan,

891 31

Örnsköldsvik, Sweden

## Orsa

## Orsa Railway Station
Järnvägsgatan,

794 30

Orsa, Sweden

## Östersund

## Östersund Central Railway Station
Stationsplan 1,

831 33 Östersund,

Sweden

## Öxnered

## Öxnered Railway Station
Öxneredsvägen 171,

462 61

Vänersborg, Sweden

# Porjus

## Porjus Railway Station

Strömgatan,

982 60

Porjus, Sweden

# Riksgränsen

## Riksgränsen Railway Station

Riksgränsvägen,

981 94

Riksgränsen, Sweden

# Röjan

## Röjan Railway Station

Röjan, Sweden

# Säffle

## Säffle Railway Station

Järnvägsgatan 12,

661 30

Säffle, Sweden

## Jämtlands Sikås

### Jämtlands Sikås Railway Station

Sikås Stationsvägen 270,

830 70

Hammerdal, Sweden

## Skellefteå

### Skellefteå Railway Station

Södra Järnvägsgatan,

931 32

Skellefteå, Sweden

## Skövde

### Skövde Central Railway Station

Stationsgatan,

541 30

Skövde, Sweden

## Slagnäs

### Slagnäs Railway Station
Järnvägsgatan,
930 91
Slagnäs, Sweden

## Söderhamn

### Söderhamn Railway Station
Söderhamnsporten 3,
826 40
Söderhamn, Sweden

## Södertälje

### Södertälje Central Railway Station
Stationsplan 1,
151 32
Södertälje, Sweden

## Södertälje Syd Railway Station

Sydgatan 1,

151 38

Södertälje, Sweden


## Sorsele

## Sorsele Railway Station

Stationsgatan,

920 70

Sorsele, Sweden


## Stockholm

## Värtahamnen Stockholm

Värtan-Terminal,

Södra Hamnvägen 46,

10 253

Stockholm, Sweden


## Stockholm Central Station

Klarabergsviadukten

72 111 64

Stockholm

**Arlanda Central Station**

Pelarganden 1D 190 60

Stockholm

**Arlanda Central Railway Station**

Arlanda Flygplats (ARN),

190 60 Stockholm-Arlanda, Sweden

**Stockholm Central Railway Station**

Centralplan,

111 64

Stockholm, Sweden

**Viking Line Terminal**

Stadsgården,

11630 Stockholm, Sweden

**Frihamnen, Magazin 2**

Tallink-Terminal,

10 253

Stockholm, Sweden

## Storlien

### Storlien Railway Station

Vintergatan,

830 19

Storlien, Sweden

## Storuman

### Storuman Railway Station

Järnvägsgatan 15,

923 31

Storuman, Sweden

## Sundsvall

### Sundsvall Central Railway Station

Landsvägsallén 6,

852 29

Sundsvall, Sweden

## Sveg

## Sveg Railway Station
Järnvägsgatan 20,
842 32
Sveg, Sweden

## Svenstavik

## Svenstavik Railway Station
Stationsvägen,
840 40
Svenstavik, Sweden

## Trelleborg

## Port of Trelleborg
Port,
231 45
Trelleborg, Sweden

## Trelleborg Central Railway Station
Kontinentplan 2,
231 42

Trelleborg, Sweden

## Täby

### Täby Centrum Railway Station
Stora Marknadsvägen,

183 34

Täby, Sweden

## Tandsjöborg

### Tandsjöborg Railway Station
820 50

Los, Sweden

## Trollhättan

### Trollhättan Central Railway Station
Bergslagstorget 1,

461 32

Trollhättan, Sweden

## Ulriksfors

**Ulriksfors Railway Station**

Ulriksfors 250,

833 93

Strömsund, Sweden

**Umeå**

**Umeå Central Railway Station**

Järnvägsallén 11,

903 28

Umeå, Sweden

**Uppsala**

**Uppsala Central Railway Station**

Olof Palmes Plats,

753 21

Uppsala, Sweden

**Visby**

**Port of Visby**

Färjeleden,

621 58

Visby, Sweden

## Vilhelmina

### Vilhelmina Railway Station

Järnvägsgatan 12,

912 34

Vilhelmina, Sweden

## Växjö

### Växjö Railway Station

Norra Järnvägsgatan,

352 33

Växjö, Sweden

## Västerås

### Västerås Central Railway Station

Södra Ringvägen 1,

722 12

Västerås, Sweden

## Varberg

### Varberg Railway Station
Västra Vallgatan,

432 41

Varberg, Sweden

## Vännäs

### Vännäs Railway Station
Östra Järnvägsgatan,

911 31

Vännäs, Sweden

## Vajkijaur

### Vajkijaur Railway Station
962 99

Jokkmokk, Sweden

## Vaggeryd

## Vaggeryd Railway Station

Stationsgatan 4,

567 30

Vaggeryd, Sweden

## Ystad

## Port of Ystad

Bornholmsgatan 2,

271 39

Ystad, Sweden

## Ystad Railway Station

Spanienfararegatan 25,

271 39

Ystad, Sweden

# Train Stations in Switzerland

## Engadin St. Moritz Mountains AG

## Betriebsleitung Train Station

Engadin St. Moritz Mountains AG

Via San Gian 30, 7500 St. Moritz

Switzerland

Phone: 081 830 00 00

## SOS Corviglia Train Station

Engadin St. Moritz Mountains AG

7500 St. Moritz

Switzerland

Phone: 081 836 50 40

## Signalbahn Train Station

Engadin St. Moritz Mountains AG

Via San Gian 30, 7500 St. Moritz

Switzerland

Phone: 081 830 00 00

## Signalstübli Train Station

Engadin St. Moritz Mountains AG

7500 St. Moritz

Switzerland

Phone: 081 833 11 38

**Corviglia-Piz Nair Luftseilbahn AG (LCPN) Train Station**

7500 St. Moritz

Switzerland

Phone: 081 833 43 44

**Schnee- und Pistenbericht des ENGADIN St. Moritz Mountain Pool Train Station**

Via San Gian 30, 7500 St. Moritz

Switzerland

Phone: 0844 84 49 44

**Grindelwald**

Luftseilbahn Pfingstegg AG Train Station

Rybigässli 25, 3818 Grindelwald

Switzerland

Phone: 033 853 26 26

## Gondelbahn Grindelwald-Männlichen AG Train Station

Grund, 3818 Grindelwald

Switzerland

Phone: 033 854 80 80


## Grindelwald BOB und WAB Train Station

3818 Grindelwald

Switzerland

Phone: 033 828 75 40


## Grindelwald Grund Train Station

3818 Grindelwald

Switzerland

Phone: 033 828 75 23


## Kandersteg

Luftseilbahn Kandersteg-Sunnbüel(Gemmi) AG Train Station

Innere Dorfstrasse 219, 3718 Kandersteg

Switzerland

Phone: 033 675 81 41

## Gondelbahn Kandersteg-Oeschinensee AG Train Station

Oeschistrasse 50, 3718 Kandersteg

Switzerland

Phone: 033 675 11 18

## Luftseilbahn Kandersteg-Allmenalp AG Train Station

Allmebahnstrasse 23, 3718 Kandersteg

Switzerland

Phone: 033 675 16 90

## Mürren

## BLM Train Station

3825 Mürren

Switzerland

Phone: 033 828 74 38

## Schilthornbahn AG Train Station

3825 Mürren

Switzerland

Phone: 033 856 21 41

## Seilbahn Mürren-Allmendhubel Train Station

Talstation, 3825 Mürren

Switzerland

Phone: 033 855 20 42

## Adelboden

## Tschentenbahnen AG Train Station

Talstation, Bellevuegässli 4, 3715 Adelboden

Switzerland

Phone: 033 673 11 06

## Bergbahnen Adelboden AG Train Station

Bonderlenstrasse 4, 3715 Adelboden

Switzerland

Phone: 033 673 90 90

## Bergbahnen Engstligenalp AG Train Station

Unter dem Birg, 3715 Adelboden

Switzerland

Phone: 033 673 32 70

## Echallens

### Administration et direction Train Station

Lausanne-Echallens-Bercher

place de la Gare 9, 1040 Echallens

Switzerland

Phone 021 886 20 00

### Administration et direction Train Station

Lausanne-Echallens-Bercher

1040 Echallens

Switzerland

Phone 021 886 20 00

### Trafic voyageurs, Service à la clientèle et vente Train Station

Lausanne-Echallens-Bercher › Gare

1040 Echallens

Switzerland

Phone 021 886 20 15

## Appels urgents Train Station
Lausanne-Echallens-Bercher

1040 Echallens

Switzerland

Phone 021 886 20 15


## Engelberg


## Bergbahnen Engelberg-Trübsee- Titlis AG (BET) Train Station
Gerschnistrasse 12, 6390 Engelberg

Switzerland

Phone 041 639 50 50


## Luftseilbahn Engelberg-Fürenalp AG Train Station
Wasserfallstrasse 222, 6390 Engelberg

Switzerland

Phone 041 637 20 94


## Unter- Obertrübsee Train Station
6390 Engelberg

Switzerland

Phone 041 637 27 25

## Grafenort

### Mettlen-Lutersee Seilbahn Train Station
Hinter Rugisbalm 1, 6388 Grafenort
Switzerland
Phone 041 637 24 33

## Interlaken

### Jungfraubahnen Train Station
Harderstrasse 14, 3800 Interlaken
Switzerland
Phone 033 828 71 11

### Schilthornbahn AG Train Station
Höheweg 2, 3800 Interlaken
Switzerland
Phone 033 826 00 07

### Drahtseilbahn Interlaken-Heimwehfluh AG Train Station

3800 Interlaken

Switzerland

Phone: 033 822 34 53


**Bahnhof BOB WAB BLM Train Station**

3822 Lauterbrunnen

Switzerland

Phone: 033 828 70 38


**BLM Train Station**

3825 Mürren

Switzerland

Phone: 033 828 74 38


**Grindelwald Grund Train Station**

3818 Grindelwald

Switzerland

Phone: 033 828 75 23


**WAB Stationsbüro Wengen Train Station**

3823 Wengen

Switzerland

Phone: 033 828 70 50

## Automatischer Strassen- Schnee- und Wetterbericht Train Station

Luftseilbahn Schwägalp-Säntis

9107 Urnäsch

Switzerland

Phone: 071 365 66 66


## Talstation Luftseilbahn Train Station

Luftseilbahn Schwägalp-Säntis

Schwägalp, 9107 Urnäsch

Switzerland

Phone: 071 365 65 65


## Berghotel Schwägalp Train Station

Luftseilbahn                    Schwägalp-Säntis

Berggasthäuser

Schwägalp, 9107 Urnäsch

Switzerland

Phone: 071 365 66 00


## Panorama-Restaurant    Säntisgipfel    Train Station

Luftseilbahn          Schwägalp-Säntis

Berggasthäuser

Säntisgipfel, 9107 Urnäsch

Switzerland

Phone: 071 277 99 55


## Gasthaus Passhöhe Schwägalp Train Station

Luftseilbahn          Schwägalp-Säntis          ›

Berggasthäuser

Beieregg, 9107 Urnäsch

Switzerland

Phone: 071 364 12 43


## Verwaltung Center Turistic Train Station

Bergbahnen Brigels Waltensburg Andiast AG

Restaurant    Curtginet,    7158    Waltensburg/Vuorz

Switzerland

Phone: 081 941 16 12

## Kasse Brigels Train Station

Bergbahnen Brigels Waltensburg Andiast
AG
Restaurant Curtginet, 7158 Waltens-
burg/Vuorz
Switzerland
Phone: 081 936 29 00


## Bergrestaurant Alp Dado Train Station

Bergbahnen Brigels Waltensburg Andiast
AG
Restaurant Curtginet, 7158 Waltens-
burg/Vuorz
Switzerland
Phone: 081 941 21 29


## Restaurant Curtginet Train Station

Bergbahnen Brigels Waltensburg Andiast
AG
7158 Waltensburg/Vuorz
Switzerland
Phone: 081 941 22 20

## Kasse Waltensburg Train Station

Bergbahnen Brigels Waltensburg Andiast
AG

7165 Breil/Brigels

Switzerland

Phone: 081 936 28 00

# Train Stations in Ukraine

**Kiev**

**Kiev Passenger Railway Station**
Vokzalna (Station) Square,
+38 (062) 319-43-09

**Darnytsia Railway Station**
3 Pryvokzalna St.,
Kiev, Ukraine
Tel: 238-4494.

**Kharkiv**

**Kharkiv Railway Station**
Kharkiv, Ukraine

**Lviv**

**Lviv Rail Terminal**
1 Dvirtseva Sq., Lviv, Ukraine, 79000
Tel:  + 38 (032) 226 2068

## Odessa

### Odessa Railway Station
Odessa in southern Ukraine

## Uzhorod

### Uzhhorod Railway Station
Uzhored Central Rail Terminal
Heorhiy Kyrpa Square
Tel: +38 (048) 727 41 33

# Train Stations in Turkey

## Adana

### Adana Central Station,
Kurtuluş Mh.,
01120
Adana, Turkey

## Afyon

### Afyon Railway Station
Ankara Railway Station

## Ankara

### Ankara Central Station,
Doğanbey Mh.,
06050
Ankara, Turkey

## Istabul

# TCDD Liman

İşletmesi Müdürlüğü Haydarpasa / Istanbul
TURKEY
Tel: 90-216-348 80 20

## Bostancı Railway Station

Bağdat Avenue,
Bostancı, Kadıköy,
Istanbul, Turkey

## Söğütlüçeşme Railway Station

Ziverbey yolu,
Kadıköy, İstanbul

## Istanbul Sirkeci Terminal

Sirkeci İstasyonu Cad.,
Eminönü, İstanbul

## İstanbul Haydarpaşa Terminal

Haydarpaşa Gar sk,
Haydarpaşa, İstanbul, Turkey
Tel: (+90) 6464249594

## Zonguldak

## Zonguldak Railway Station

Karaelmas Mh.,
 67020
Zonguldak, Turkey

## Adaparzari

## Gar meydanı

54100 Semerciler,
Sakarya Turkey

## Balı kesir

## Balı kesir Railway Station

Tel: (+90-266) 713 60 89 - 715 30 50

## Bandı rma

## Bandı rma Railway Station

Kaşif Acar Cd, 10200 Balı kesir, Turkey
Tel: +90 (212) 455 6900

+90 266 714 3482

## Eskişehir

### Eskişehir Central Station

Kütahya yolu, Tepebaşı,

Eskişehir 26140

Turkey

## Gaziantep

### Gaziantep Railway Station

İstasyon Cd, Gaziantep Cd,

Gaziantep, Turkey

Tel : (+90)3422110030

## İzmir

### İzmir Alsancak Terminal

Konak, Şehitler Cd,

2-10, 35230

Umurbey, İzmir 34726

## İzmir Basmane Terminal

İzmit Railway Station

İstasyon Cd, Kozluk Mh, İzmit

Tel: 0262-311 2311

## Torbali Railway Station,

Tepeköy Mh.,

Ağalar Cd No:1, 35860

İzmir, Turkey

Tel: +90 232 856 1742

## Kars

## Kars Railway Station

Bayram Acar Sk, Kars, Turkey

## Mersin

## Mersin Railway Station

Yunuskent Mh.,

Şht. Ahmet Yılmaz

Cd No:1 D:94,

33090

Merkez, Turkey

Tel:+90 324 238 6560

## Sarı kamı ş

**Sarı kamı ş Railway Station,**

Kars-Sarı kamı ş Yolu,

Sarı kamı ş, Turkey.

## Tarsus

**Tarsus Railway Station**

Karden Langen Blv. Tarsus

## Yenice

**Yenice Railway Station**

stasyon Sk, Yenice

# Train Stations in United Kingdom

## Abbey wood Train Station

Address: Wilton Road, Abbey Wood

London, SE2 9RH

London, United Kingdom.

Phone: 0845 000 2222

## Acton Central Railway Station

Address: Churchfield Road, Acton

London, W3 6BD

London, United Kingdom.

Phone: 0870 512 5240

## Acton Main Line Station

Address: Horn Lane, Acton

London, W3 0BP

London, United Kingdom.

Phone: 0845 700 0125

## Alexandra Palace Station

Address: 157 Station Road, Wood Green

London, N22 7SS

London, United Kingdom.
Phone: 0845 026 4700

## Anerley Railway Station
Address: Anerley Station Road, Penge
London, SE20 8PT
London, United Kingdom.
Phone: 0845 127 2920

## Angel Road Station
Address: Angel Road, London
Angel Road, Edmonton
London, N18 3AY
London, United Kingdom.
Phone: 0845 600 7245

## Balham Train Station
Address: Balham Station Road, Balham
London, SW12 9SG
London, United Kingdom.
Phone: 0845 127 2920

## Barking Train Station

Address: Station Parade, Town Centre

Barking, IG11 8TU

London, United Kingdom.

Phone: 0845 601 4873


**Barnes Railway Station**

Address: Rocks Lane, Barnes

London, SW13 0DG

London, United Kingdom.

Phone: 0845 748 4950


**Battersea Park Railway Station**

Address: Battersea Park Road, Battersea

London, SW11 3BH

London, United Kingdom.

Phone: 0845 748 4950


**Beckenham Junction Station**

Address: Station Approach, New Beckenham

Beckenham, BR3 1HY

London, United Kingdom.

Phone: 0845 000 2222

## Bellingham Railway Station

Address: Randlesdown Road, Bellingham

London, SE6 3BT

London, United Kingdom.

Phone: 0845 000 2222

## Belmont Station

Address: Railway Approach

Brighton Road,

Sutton, SM2 6BH

London, United Kingdom.

Phone: 0845 127 2920

## Bethnal Green Station

Address: Three Colts Lane, Bethnal Green

London, E2 6JL

London, United Kingdom.

Phone: 0845 600 7245

## Bexleyheath Station

Address: Station Road, Town Centre

Bexleyheath, DA7 4AA

London, United Kingdom.
Phone: 0845 000 2222

**Bickley Station**
Address: Southborough Road, Town Centre
Bromley, BR1 2EB
London, United Kingdom.
Phone: 0845 000 2222

**Bowes Park Station**
Address: Myddleton Road, Bowes Park
London, N22 8NL
London, United Kingdom.
Phone: 0845 026 4700

**Brixton Railway Station**
Address: 32 Brixton Station Road, Brixton
London, SW9 8PE
London, United Kingdom.
Phone: 0845 748 4950

**Brimsdown Station**

Address: Green Street, Ponders End
Enfield, EN3 7NA
London, United Kingdom.
Phone: 0845 600 7245

## Brondesbury Park Railway Station

Address:  Brondesbury Park, Kilburn
London, NW6 7TT
London, United Kingdom.
Phone: 0845 748 4950

## Bruce Grove Station

Address: High Road, White Hart Lane
London, N17 8AD
London, United Kingdom.
Phone: 0845 600 7245

## Brondesbury Railway Station

Address: Kilburn High Road, Hampstead
London, NW6 7QB
London, United Kingdom.
Phone: 0845 748 4950

## Bush Hill Park Railway Station

Address: St. Marks Road, Enfield Town

Enfield, EN1 1BA

London, United Kingdom.

Phone: 0845 600 7245


## Caledonian Road & Barnsbury Station

Address: Caledonian Road, Islington

London, N1 1DN

London, United Kingdom.

Phone: 0845 601 4867


## Cambridge Heath Station

Address: Hackney Road, Bethnal Green

London, E2 7NA

London, United Kingdom.

Phone: 0845 600 7245


## Camden Road Station

Address: Bonny Street, King's Cross

London, NW1 9LQ. London, United Kingdom.

Phone: 0845 601 4867

## Canonbury Railway Station

Address: St. Pauls Road, Islington

London, N1 2LY. London, United Kingdom.

Phone: 0845 748 4950

## Carpenders Park Mainline Station

Address: Station Approach

Prestwick Road, Town Centre

Watford, WD19 6LH

London, United Kingdom.

Phone: 0845 601 4867

## Castle Bar Park Station

Address: Copley Close, Hanwell

London, W7 1BB

London, United Kingdom.

Phone: 0845 700 0125

## Catford Bridge Railway Station

Address: Catford Bridge, Catford

London, SE6 4RE

London, United Kingdom.
Phone: 0845 000 2222

**Chadwell Heath Railway Station**
Address: Station Road, Chadwell Heath
Romford, RM6 4BE
London, United Kingdom.
Phone: 0845 600 7245

**Charlton Station**
Charlton Church Lane, Charlton
London, SE7 7AB
London, United Kingdom.
Phone: 0845 000 2222

**Clapton Station**
Address: Upper Clapton Road, Lower
Clapton
London, E5 9JP
London, United Kingdom.
Phone: 0845 600 7245

**Claygate Station**

Address: Station Approach

The Parade, Town Centre

Esher, KT10 0PB

London, United Kingdom.

Phone: 0845 600 0650


**Coulsdon Town Railway Station**

Address: Station Approach, Town Centre

Coulsdon, CR5 2YB

London, United Kingdom.

Phone: 0845 127 2920


**Crayford Station**

Address: Lower Station Road, Crayford

Dartford, DA1 3PY

London, United Kingdom.

Phone: 0845 000 2222


**Cricklewood Railway Station**

Address: Cricklewood Lane, Cricklewood

London, NW2 1HL

London, United Kingdom.

Phone: 0845 748 4950

## Custom House Railway Station
Address: Victoria Dock Road, Newham
London, E16 3BX
London, United Kingdom.
Phone: 0845 601 4867

## Dalston Junction Station
Address: 2 Dalston Lane, Dalston
London, E8 3DE
London, United Kingdom.
Phone: 020 7222 1234

## Deptford Station
Address: Deptford High Street, Deptford
London, SE8 3NU
London, United Kingdom.
Phone: 0845 000 2222

## Drayton Green Station
Address: Drayton Bridge Road,
London, W13
London, United Kingdom.

Phone: 0845 700 0125

## Devons Road Train Station

Address: Devons Road, Mile End

London, E3 3QX

London, United Kingdom.

Phone: 0845 748 4950

## Ealing Broadway Station

Address: Haven Green, Ealing

London, W5 2UP

London, United Kingdom.

Phone: 0845 700 0125

## Eden Park Railway Station

Address: Upper Elmers End Road, Elmers

End

Beckenham, BR3 3HQ

London, United Kingdom.

Phone: 0845 000 2222

## East Dulwich Station

Address: Grove Vale, Dulwich

London, SE22 8EF

London, United Kingdom.

Phone: 0845 127 2920


**Eltham Railway Station**

Address: Well Hall Road, Eltham

London, SE9 6SL

London, United Kingdom.

Phone: 0845 000 2222


**Elephant & Castle Railway Station**

Address: Elephant Road, Walworth

London, SE17 1LB

London, United Kingdom.

Phone: 0845 026 4700


**Fenchurch Street Railway Station**

Address: Fenchurch Street, The City

London, EC3M 4AJ

London, United Kingdom.

Phone: 0845 748 4950


**First Capital Connect**

Address: Old Street Underground Station
St. Agnes Well, The City
London, EC1Y 1BE
London, United Kingdom.
Phone: 0845 026 4700

**Forest Gate Train Station**
Address: Woodgrange Road, Forest Gate
London, E7 0QH
London, United Kingdom.
0845 600 7245

**Fulwell Station**
Address: Wellington Gardens, Fulwell
Twickenham, TW2 5NY
London, United Kingdom.
Phone: 084 5600 0650

**Gidea Park Station**
Address:Station Road, Town Centre
Romford, RM2 6BX
London, United Kingdom.
Phone: 0845 600 7245

**Gospel Oak Railway Station**

Address:Gordon    House    Road,    Kentish
Town

London, NW5 1LT

London, United Kingdom.

Phone: 0845 601 4867

# Section 4 – The Wonders of Europe

## The Colosseum of Rome (Italy)

Undeniably, one of the most famous locations in Rome is the Colosseum, which was used as an amphitheater in 80 AD. A feat of architecture and ingenious engineering has made the Colosseum endure the duress of time. This spectacular, circular arena could house around 50,000 to 80,000 spectators and functioned as a theatre for gladiator fights, executions, hunting animals, or classical plays.

UNESCO has allotted it the status of World Heritage site because it has become an emblem for the imperial powers of Rome. The Colosseum underwent great depreciation due to the advent of Christianity in this region, which saw it as a barbaric edifice. The design of the Colosseum and the symmetry in arches and squares is almost baffling to modern day architects. With its different types of columns, windows, gilded shields, painted statues, and huge porticoes, it was a stately piece of art for that era.

The arena was covered with sand and had trap doors which allowed wild animals to enter the fight suddenly. A dark basement was also added later to keep the slaves, fighters, and animals in drudgery and suspense. Today, the Colosseum stands in a perplexing mixture of ruin and glory and is still a famous tourist destination as it evokes memories of a bygone era which was extravagant in both its prosperity and brutality.

## Pompeii in Southern Italy

Pompeii was a prosperous and well-to-do Roman city, the history of which was built through backward induction and archeological explorations in this region. It was discovered in 1748 that the location was inhabited by people and was a properly functioning city until the volcanic eruption of Mount Vesuvius in 79 AD burned everything to ashes and covered it in a thick layer of pumice and ash.

Around 20,000 people were living in this area at the time, out of which 2,000 failed to evacuate in time and died due to the eruption. The idea of Pompeii is tragic and poignantly miserable for those who were taken unaware by a disaster of such tremendous consequence. Pompeii derived its fame from its rediscovery by many archeologists who found very well preserved artifacts and objects that provide a gainful insight into the lives of people.

It is fascinating to uncover the relics, which provide a window into the lives of people in the first century, because their life has been preserved exactly the way it was on that ill-fated day. The initial accounts of this city were obtained from Pliny the Younger who recounted seeing the eruption firsthand. Currently, Pompeii has earned the status of a World Heritage site from UNESCO and it receives millions of visitors who are drawn to its mysterious and enigmatic history. It remains one of the most visited sites in Italy and has doubtlessly become one of the Wonders of Europe with its rich cultural and historical background.

# Acropolis in Athens (Greece)

The Acropolis of Athens is an area which houses several historically and culturally important buildings of Ancient Greece. It is also an emblem of the beautifully-mastered architectural innovation. The monuments symbolize classical Greek Antiquity and serve as an inspiration for archeologists, historians, writers, and tourists. The Acropolis includes the Parthenon, the Propylaia, the Erechtheion, and the temple of Athena Nike. While some of these sites were destroyed by wars, the ruins still remain as reminders of a glorious past.

The building of the Acropolis was ordained by the statesman Pericles under the guidance of the sculptor Pheidias. The rocky hill was converted into intricately fashioned buildings of marble and stone. The impressive fact about the Acropolis is that it was built in $5^{th}$ Century B.C. and it has miraculously survived in the shape that it is today. UNESCO also assigned it the World Heritage site label, which allows for its better preservation and care. The site

at which Acropolis now stands was not
made by Pericles; rather it existed as early as 6,000 BC and was continuously built
upon by following generations.

After the Greeks, it was under Roman,
Byzantine, Latin, and Ottoman control. The
legacy of Greece was somewhat restored
after the Greek war of independence. The
buildings have been restored by recon-
structing the original designs and trying to
nullify the centuries of impact of war, pol-
lution, and disrepair. Today it is listed as
a special monument in the European Cultural Heritage list and tourists flock from
all around the globe to view these majestic structures.

# The Alhambra in Granada (Spain)

The city of Granada is graced by the presence of the monumental structure known as Alhambra. Alhambra has evolved to become a grand palace and fortress complex but when it was originally built the fortress was small and unassuming. Mohammed ben Al-Ahmar and later Yusuf I, Sultan of Granada built over it. The Alhambra is a remnant of the legacy of the Muslim rule in Spain.

The Alhambra represents the peak of Muslim glory and represents Islamic architecture in perfection. It has been termed as a World Heritage site by UNESCO as well. The structure and form of this area was also influenced by Europeans in the following years. For instance, the Duke of Wellington added the English Elms due to which a sharp color contrast was created between the pearl-like palace and the deep-set green trees.

Alhambra is also popular for its natural beauty: flowers, birds and greenery embellish this area and enhance its beauty. The basic idea behind the creation of Alhambra was to build paradise on Earth and therefore, the presence of fountains, pools, gardens and its inscriptions all refer to the Muslim ideal of heaven. Arabic calligraphy, carving, and painted tiles adorn the walls of the palace, along with the beautiful artwork and carvings on the ceiling, arches and arabesques.

Surprisingly enough, Alhambra as it stands today did not follow a single architectural plan, and structures and decorations were added with time. As a tourist destination it is highly popular because people can see the change in dynasties from Muslims to Christians embodied in Alhambra.

# Hagia Sophia in Istanbul (Turkey)

Hagia Sophia is a present day tourist attraction located in the heartland of Turkey, the nexus of Eastern and Western cultures melding together. The word means 'Holy Wisdom' and doubtlessly tourists feel a sense of spiritual elation upon viewing this architectural feat. It was named after Saint Sophia to symbolize the Holy Wisdom of Christianity.

The sands of time modified the Hagia Sophia consequentially. Initially it was built by the Byzantines as an orthodox Green church and later, with the advent of the Ottomans it became a splendid royal mosque. On its initial conception it was built in the honor of Logos or 'Christ as the reason or the Holy Word'. It functioned as a cathedral for thousands of years and the dome of Hagia Sophia was designed by the Byzantines. The original church dates back to 532 AD.

Turkish leader Mehmed II transformed it into a mosque after gaining power and a strong flavor of Muslim art and architecture was incorporated into this majestic cathedral. The images of Jesus and Mary were painted and plastered over to efface the presence of Christianity. Today Hagia Sophia is a UNESCO World Heritage site and is a popular destination to experience a wondrous synthesis of Muslim and Christian religion, culture and architecture.

# Stonehenge in Amesbury (England)

One of the most enigmatic structures of this world, for which no accurate explanation can be gathered, stands proudly in a green field in Amesbury, England. Stonehenge is an ancient, megalithic monument which had ritualistic significance for the inhabitants of the prehistoric era. It consists of a series of large stones standing erect in a circle. The ingenious design of the Stonehenge comprises 100 menhirs and a total of 180 large standing stones.

These holy places were built for ceremonial or funerary purposes. Its architectural design and arrangement of stones is highly fascinating for historians, architects, and archeologists. The concentric plan and the shaping of the structures using stone and earth have baffled people because this structure has been standing on the face of earth from 3,000 or 2,000 BC. The word Stonehenge describes its structure of the stones hinging on other stones, in an L-shaped formation.

The mystery that surrounds the presence of this unusual structure attracts tourists and adventurers alike. Some of the explanations for its structure include conjecture that it might have been built for astronomical reasons. Today it represents the prehistoric culture and the evolution of engineering in that era, along with the surrounding structures. Stonehenge is listed amongst the Wonders of the World and is a part of our collective heritage because it helps us gain valuable insight into the lives of people who lived in the Neolithic and Bronze Age.

# St. Basil's Cathedral

If you've ever seen a postcard of Moscow, a poster, a picture, or even a souvenir shop trinket, you'll recognize the familiar yet colorful sight of asymmetrical spires and cylinders rising out of a pleasantly erratic structure. This spectacular sight is the crown jewel of Moscow's architecture: St. Basil's Cathedral.

St. Basil's Cathedral, also known as the 'Cathedral of the Intercession of the Virgin by the Moat,' is famous for its unique church structure as well as its seemingly erratic design. The Cathedral was built upon the instructions of Ivan the Terrible in 1555, as a commemoration of his military victory. The Kazan forces had been captured from the Mongols, and Ivan wanted the entire world to see his brute force represented in the most unique church in Europe. A popular urban myth states that Ivan later had the church's architect blinded so that he may never be able to build anything more striking.

The Cathedral is open for visitors daily, except for Tuesday, from 11 am to 5:30pm. Inside, the collection of art, century's old architecture, and the church itself are all enough to keep visitors occupied and inspired for the day. The various doors, steps, and intricate designs reflect the tumultuous and rich religious history of Russia. For anyone interested in viewing the cathedral from outside only, it's accessible at all times, as long as the Red Square is open. Once a year, on the Day of the Intercession in October, the cathedral holds its annual service.

The FPK (Federal Passenger Company) operates train travel throughout most of Russia. Tourists may buy tickets in English and take a route going through the Red Square. The closest train stations are Borovitskaya and Biblioteka imeni Lenina.

## Neuschwanstein Castle

Neuschwanstein Castle in southern Bavaria is one of Germany's many artistic gifts to the world. Its otherworldly scenic beauty, rich history, fascinating architecture, and idyllic location attract curious visitors from all over the world on an annual basis. Traveling to Neuschwanstein is more than a tourist experience; it's an adventure through Germany's beauty, olden times, and culture.

Construction began in 1869 as something of a private retreat for King Ludwig the II, who used to return to the confines of the castle and take time away from public life. The castle did not become publically accessible until 7 weeks after the King's death. What is today a massively popular tourist site was once the King's most clandestine retreat, perhaps this is one of the reasons why Neuschwanstein is often referred to as 'the castle of the fairy tale king.'

Tourist traffic is remarkably high, especially in the summer months when the castle receives over 6,000 visitors a day. Trained guides–who speak fluent English–take individual and group walking tours throughout the impressive structure, and are well versed in the rich history of the region.

The simplest train route is through the town of Fussen, where bus 9713 will drop you off in Hohenschwangau. The castle is a 30-minute walk from Hohenschwangau, but for added romanticism, take a horse-drawn carriage ride up the hill and give yourself at least 3 hours to spend exploring the wonders. Be sure to see all the swans, including the swan sink, and learn the reason it is called "New Swan Stone."

# St. Peter's Basilica

As the official smallest nation in the world, Vatican City is a remarkable representation of the tumultuous history of Christianity. At the heart of this unique land is the world's largest church, St. Peter's Basilica. St. Peter was considered Jesus' 'rock,' and the first official Pope of the Roman Catholic Church, and it is upon his metaphoric shoulders that much of modern Christianity has developed.

St. Peter's Basilica sprawls across Vatican Hill, at the exact location where St. Peter was martyred in 64 AD. It was built there by the 4$^{th}$ century emperor Constantine, who wanted the basilica built around the remote shrine then dedicated to St. Peter. By 329 AD, St. Peter's Basilica was completed and its longest nave stood nearly 280 meters high. Since initial construction, some of Rome's most famed architects and artists have contributed to expanding the design of the original structure. Today, the church represents the history of religious art as much as it does religion itself.

St. Peter's Basilica is one of the most revered tourist sites in the world, millions of Christians flock together every month of the year to spend time in this intimidating place. Adding to the charm of the church is St. Peter's Square, the partially enclosed esplanade that visitors pass through on their way to the church. Once inside

St. Peter's Basilica, tourists have a wonderful view of the square outside.

By train, St. Peter's Basilica is a short ride toward Battistini, at the Ottaviano-S. Pietro exit. From there, the St. Peter's Square is a short walk south on Via Ottaviano. St. Peter's Basilica is open for mass every day and special masses take place from 9 am to 6 pm on Sundays. Entrance is completely free for visitors, but a strict dress code is enforced on both males and females.

# Sistine Chapel

If you're planning a visit to the Vatican and St. Peter's Basilica, your trip will be incomplete without a visit to the famed Sistine chapel. A part of the official papal residence, the Sistine chapel has immense historic, artistic, and religious significance. It is the 'room' in which every papal conclave takes place and is considered the official 'papal chapel.' Through history, it has also been a private prayer and relaxation space reserved for the esteemed Cardinals.

Its significance as a tourist attraction has increased due to the famous artwork that adorns its ceilings and walls. In May 1508, under the commission of Pope Paul III, Roman artist and sculptor Michelangelo signed a contract to restore the chapel ceiling. His greatest contribution was his collection of frescoes and his painting, 'The Last Judgment,' a gargantuan work of art that scales the entire wall behind the alter of the Sistine chapel. Despite the controversial history of the artwork, it rose to incredible fame relatively quickly and 'The Last Judgement' is one of the main reasons the Sistine Chapel has gained such prominence amongst tourists.

The Sistine chapel is a part of the Vatican Museums and is open to visitors during tourist hours. It's only a 10-minute walk from the main entrance and its structure may also be viewed from across St. Peter's Square. Sunday mass is a sight to behold for churchgoers, but any other day of the week is also a guaranteed good time.

# Louvre

The Musee du Louvre is perhaps the international symbol of French civilization and culture. One of the largest and most famous art galleries in the world, the Louvre is home to over 35,000 of the greatest masterpieces of artistic creation in the history of mankind.

As the most visited museum on earth, the Louvre has a lot more to offer than a traditional art collection; it is a work of art in itself and has a story to match. The museum's permanent collection includes a wide variety of religious and cultural art. From Egyptian antiquities and Islamic Sculptures to Decorative art and Da Vinci's 'Mona Lisa,' there is something for everyone at the Musee du Louvre.

The only thing that may possibly overshadow the overwhelming collection of art is the sheer size of the museum. Estimates suggest that it would take the average visitor nearly 3 weeks to take in all the art that encompasses the nearly 61,000 square meter area. While such dedication may be common, it is hardly possible for a tourist to get through the staggering collection in a mere day.

The museum offers a wide range of self-guided tours that last up to 2 hours, along with official museum tours conducted in both English and French. The Louvre is open on Monday and Thursday from 9am to 6pm, Wednesday and Friday from 9am to 10pm. It is closed on Tuesdays, Christmas, and the 1$^{st}$ of December. The area is easily accessible by subway, and the closest Paris Metro Station is the *Louvre* Rivoli and Palais Royal Musée du *Louvre on the yellow line.*

# Palace of Versailles

The 'Chateau de Versailles' is the central structure of the Palace that was the official government residence during the reigns of Kings Louis XIV, XV, and XVI between 1682 and 1790. The French monarchy kept the palace at their personal and professional disposal. It was the place where they arranged secret trysts with their mistresses, contemplated coups, and made the decisions that have come to shape European history.

While the monarchs are long gone and the palace has not been an official residence since the French Revolution, it's an integral part of the French government. The classic architecture of the building is complemented by the lavish surrounding gardens. Visitors often spend the majority of their time strolling through the sprawling gardens, admiring the fountains and vast flowerbeds. These gardens are a magnificent sight during the spring and summer months, though they are open to visitors throughout the year.

The Palace is open for tourists all week—except Monday—from 9am onwards. The buildings are closed on Mondays but the gardens are still accessible. Visitors may take a train in from Paris and stop at the Versailles Rive Gauche Station, a 5-minute walk from the palace. There is also a train from Paris Saint Lazare to Versailles Rive Droite, and one between Paris Montpar-

nasse and Versailles Chantiers. Both stations are a picturesque 10-15-minute walk
from the palace.

# Canals of Venice

Imagine gliding down a canal under the shimmering Venice moonlight, possibly serenaded by a musical gondola driver. This isn't just a romantic tourist experience; it's the way of life in this beautiful Italian city. The 150 canals of Venice are the streets and roads of the city; there is no room for land passenger vehicles. The only way to travel throughout the city is by foot or canal vehicle.

Fugitive inhabitants originally built these canals in the 5$^{th}$ century, aiming to inhabit a lagoon-like city and avoid the barbaric onslaughts of invaders. Soon, however, they became a way of life and the way of life has not changed much ever since.

Although most of Venice is composed of hundreds of interconnected canals, the Grand Canal is the only large one. It is about 3 kilometers long and connects to hundreds of smaller subsidiary canals. A ride through the Grand Canal offers a magnificent view of the Rialto Bride and the many renaissance-style structures that line the cobbled streets.

Tourists may explore the city on foot by taking one of over 400 pedestrian bridges or use a water transport vehicle. While the Gondola ride is also a classic, many visitors prefer to live like locals and take one of the islands' 'water buses' known as

'Vaporettos.' The Vaporetto moves swiftly through the canals and is the preferred method of transportation for most locals. In contrast, the slow mystique of the gondola has increased its charm as a tourist attraction.

# Italian Riviera

The Italian Riviera has an old-world charm, a certain allure that provides luxury and comfort to visitors. Its scenic beauty, sweeping shores, and crystal blue ocean waters have enchanted many a visitor. Even literary giants like Ernest Hemmingway and Ezra Pound used to retreat to the Italian Coast for some peace, relaxation, and inspiration.

The Italian Riviera is composed mainly of the coast of Liguria, to the west of the great boot. It is home to many lazy seaside towns and fishing villages. The most popular is Portofino, Italy's largest fishing village. Portofino is a favorite vacation spot for the rich and famous and has developed to cater to the needs of the fabulously wealthy. Ritzy restaurants and yachts dot the coastline through the summer months.

But there's a great deal more to the region than just Hollywood glamor; some of Italy's finest churches, history, and art reside in the wonderful city of Genova. Tourists can take a break from the sun, sea, and sand to explore the ornate palazzos and medieval monuments—all on a budget.

The eclectic local markets, delicious seafood, and wine are just some of the many must-see attractions along the Italian Riviera. Best of all, this haven may just be a train away.

# Best Cities to Visit in Europe

Europe is a treasure trove of beauty, culture, and history. One lifetime is probably not enough to explore the vast and diverse landscapes of this fascinating continent. So the best places to start are often the most popular ones. Here are some of the best cities to visit in Europe:

### Copenhagen, Denmark

There's a reason the Danish consistently rank amongst the happiest people in the world; there is much to appreciate about the fulfilling culture of Denmark. As the capital, Copenhagen is the hub for political and cultural development. It is one of the most beautiful and developed cities in Europe, and still manages to maintain an eco-friendly outlook and lifestyle. With almost 50% of the city residents being bicycle commuters, the city is known for its limited energy consumption and active lifestyle. People in Copenhagen truly enjoy their city; they drink in the sights and breathe in the fresh air. Tourists can do the same, whilst enjoying the scrumptious Nordic cuisine and local wine. Take in some of the culture at the Copenhagen Jazz Festival and the Louisiana Museum of Modern Art.

### Bern, Switzerland

Move over, Zurich and Geneva. Bern is another European capital that breaks through the stereotype and shows its visitors the time of their life. Bern is home to the collision between old and new; new technology and modern architectural design meets the vintage elegance of the Old City.

A UNESCO World Heritage Site, Bern's Old town boasts of some scrumptious local cuisine and fashionable boutiques. This is the city Albert Einstein once lived in; this is the city that rules one of the most peaceful and progressive nations on the planet.

**Budapest, Hungary**

Budapest is a unique city in an already unique continent. It is a combination of the exotic East and the eclectic West. Along the beautiful Danube, Budapest is a glittering hub of lively gardens, classic architecture, and trendy restaurants. This city welcomes the young and the old to drink in the experience. Budapest's famous Szechenyi thermal baths have been around since the 16th century and are perhaps the nation's most popular tourist site.

Visitors to Budapest can spend their time lazing about in one of the local coffee shops and try traditional Hungarian cuisine, or dine in a glitzy five star restaurant for some special treatment. Either way, Budapest will be an experience to remember.

## Marseille, France

Marseille has progressed fast and far. Marseilles offers its visitor a glimpse of France that cannot be found anywhere else. Its fishing history makes it the place for the world's best seafood, where visitors have a choice between the local fare and more upscale fine dining. Marseille has a range of assorted markets and shops lining the winding streets, and the 19th century architecture is a world on its own. For a low-key, culture-filled, and thrilling vacation, there are no cities that set the standard like Marseille does.

## Natural Wonders of Europe

Europe has quite the collection of natural wonders; from rivers and glaciers to geographic anomalies, the continent is as diverse as it is beautiful. Here are some of the fascinating natural wonders.

# Dolomites, Italy

A representation of the rugged beauty of northern Italy, the Dolomites are a series of mountains above 2,000 meters, with 18 of the mountains rising higher than 3,000 meters. They provide a stunning backdrop to a major portion of the northern Italian region and are a great vacation spot for anyone interested in some physical activity. The temperate climate allows for a variety of activities such as hiking, paragliding, mountain biking, and jogging. Visitors can also take steel cables up along the Via Ferratas and spend some time enjoying the gorgeous view from above. Perhaps the greatest thing about spending time in the Dolomites is how easy it is to travel to and from; it is a little over an hour away from the city of Verona.

# Fjords of Norway

Norway isn't just known for its extreme climates, it is also the location of most of the world's most fascinating fjords. Visitors are greeted with the sight of breathtakingly blue water and raw, green fjords dotted around. For a better look at the fjords, take a boat cruise around the water to revel in the beauty and serenity of the place. The Fjords are most easily accessible by train; the ride to the Flam station (the trainstop nearest to the Aurlandfjord)

has been named by Lonely Planet as one of 'The Top Scenic Train Journeys of Europe.' A trip to the fjords is the perfect way to top off your rail adventure through Europe.

## Northern Lights, Sweden

The Aurora Borealis is an unforgettable sight; the energy of those Northern Lights dancing around and lighting up the world around them is well worth the journey to Abisko. Sweden. Abisko is a remote city, a nearly 20 hour train ride away from Stockholm. But the night-time view is in-imitable and the journey there is an enjoy-able one. Especially during the winter and early spring, the weather is just the right amount of chilly and the mountains are beautifully snow-capped. The best way to reach Abisko is via night train, first from Stockholm to Boden and from there, through the town of Kiruna to Abisko.

# Krimml, Austria

The Krimml Falls is a series of heart stopping waterfalls near the Hohe Tauern National Park in northern Austria. Austria's highest waterfall crashes through the cliffs of Krimml at nearly 400 meters high and is a unique sensory experience for any visitor. Aside from gazing mesmerized at the roaring burst of waves through the fall, tourists may spend their time exploring a series of hiking trails through Hohe Tauern National park. The backdrop of glaciers and snowy mountains will leave you speechless and introduce you to one of the most beautiful sights you may ever see.

# Cliffs of Moher, Ireland

To visitors' confusion, the Cliffs of Moher are also colloquially known as the Cliffs of Coher. Linguistic perplexity aside, they represent everything feral and beautiful about Ireland. Located in the southwestern region of Ireland, the Cliffs of Moher are a series of sandstone and hale structures that rise out land up to heights of 700 feet. Most interesting about this region is the biodiversity, currently over 32,000 birds, representing 30 different species inhabit the cliffs. Explorers are welcome to witness one of the most awe-inspiring sites Europe has to offer.

# Thermal Springs, Italy

Hungary is better known for the thermal springs, but Italy is never to be outdone. The Thermal springs of the Tuscan Region are Italy's best-kept secret, located near the town of Saturina, deep between two warm waterfalls; the springs are open for tourists throughout the year and at no charge whatsoever. They are wildly beautiful and rumored to date back to over 2,000 years ago. Steeped in history and yet modern: that's the definition of Italy.

Take a train to Albinia, and then two bus-es, one from Albinia to Manciano and an-other 30-minute bus to Saturina. Enjoy the beautiful view during your bus ride there.

## Davolja Varos, Serbia

Davolja Varos is the name of a rock formation located in southern Serbia. The result of excessive erosion and weathering, over 200 unique rock structures are littered across the Radan Mountains. Visitors may hike along the mountain to view these beautiful, erratic structures rise up from within the plush greenery of the mountainside.

The surrounding space is also home to two mineral-rich natural springs. The 'Crveno Vrelo' spring is deep and acidic, as is the 'Djavola Voda.' The interesting thing about Davolja Varos is that it is a geographically unique region; the dryness of the cliffs and the acidity of the spring water create a unique environment...one that is easily accessible by foot and not too far from the nearest city.

# Conclusion

I hope you have enjoyed reading about traveling through Europe by train. If you feel I have missed something important, please let me know. You can contact me through my website BlueMarbleXpress.com.

I also have The Ultimate North America Train Travel book and The Ultimate Asia Train Travel book (due out April 2014).

J. DOYLE WHITE

54512061R00230

Made in the USA
Lexington, KY
18 August 2016